Opera
Guide

21

The Valkyrie
Die Walküre
Wagner

Linda Esther Gray as Sieglinde and Gwyneth Jones as Brünnhilde in the production by Götz Friedrich at Covent Garden in 1982 (photo: Reg Wilson)

Preface

This series, published under the auspices of English National Opera and The Royal Opera, aims to prepare audiences to enjoy and evaluate opera performances. Each book is the product of many hands. The Guides to *The Ring of the Nibelung* contain Wagner's text and the translation by Andrew Porter, with a list of musical leitmotifs. The accompanying essays have been commissioned to give an insight into each work, as well as a perspective on the cycle as a whole.

ENO is most grateful to National Westminster Bank for sponsoring *The Ring* Guides, as well as the new production of the cycle. This sponsorship which has already supported Opera Guides and productions of *Fidelio* and *The Mastersingers of Nuremberg* forms part of the Bank's wide-ranging programme of community service.

Nicholas John
Series Editor

21

The Valkyrie
Die Walküre

Richard Wagner

Opera Guide Series Editor: Nicholas John

Published in association with
English National Opera and The Royal Opera
This Guide is sponsored by ♻ **National Westminster Bank**

John Calder · London
Riverrun Press · New York

First published in Great Britain, 1983, by
John Calder (Publishers) Ltd,
18 Brewer Street,
London W1R 4AS

and

First published in the U.S.A., 1983, by
Riverrun Press Inc.,
175 Fifth Avenue,
New York, NY 10010

BRITISH LIBRARY CATALOGUING IN PUBLICATION DATA
Wagner, Richard, *1813-1883*
    The Valkyrie.—(Opera guide; 21)
    1. Wagner, Richard, *1813-1883*. Walküre, Die
    2. Operas—Librettos
    I. Title   II. John, Nicholas   III. Series
    782.1'092'4   ML410.W14

    Library of Congress Catalogue Card Number: 83-045245

ISBN 0-7145-4019-6

John Calder (Publishers) Ltd., English National Opera and The Royal Opera House, Covent Garden Ltd., receive financial assistance from the Arts Council of Great Britain. English National Opera also receives financial assistance from the Greater London Council.

Typeset in Plantin by Margaret Spooner Typesetting, Dorchester, Dorset.

Printed and bound in Great Britain at The Camelot Press Ltd, Southampton

Contents

List of Illustrations

A Conflict of Power and Love

Geoffrey Skelton

Quite apart from its function within the *Ring* cycle as a whole, *The Valkyrie* has always enjoyed a separate existence as a work on its own, and the reason for that is not difficult to see. Its story of two ill-fated lovers and a daughter who defies her powerful father in her effort to help them is one that appeals directly to our emotions, and Wagner himself was as much moved by this aspect of the drama as the rest of us. When he decided, after writing the text of his two Siegfried dramas, to depict the events leading up to them in action, instead of merely narrating them, he told Liszt (in a letter of November 20, 1851) that it was not merely dramatic expediency that had persuaded him to extend his work, but also enthusiasm over the extraordinarily rich dramatic material: 'Think of the wonderful, yet disastrous love between Siegmund and Siegelind [Sieglinde]; Wodan [Wotan] in his deeply mysterious involvement in this love; then in his discord with Fricka, in his raging self-discipline as, in the interests of propriety, he proclaims Siegmund's death; and finally the splendid Valkyrie, Brünhilde [Brünnhilde], as, guessing Wodan's innermost thoughts, she defies the god and is punished by him.'

Wagner's decision to extend the work had the effect of radically changing the balance of his original plan, supplanting Siegfried as the central character of his Nibelung drama and putting the god Wotan in his place. What had begun as a work about the German national hero had now become a vast cosmic drama, in which a god obsessed with power is forced by his inadequacy to will his own destruction.

In his prose draft 'The Nibelung Myth as Sketch for a Drama' (which he wrote in 1848 before starting *Siegfried's Death* and *Young Siegfried*) Wagner outlined Wotan's sinful theft of power (symbolised by Alberich's ring), his immediate loss of it to the giants, and his realisation that, having disqualified himself by his sin, he must delegate his function to a new and uncompromised order — the human race. The outcome of his efforts to achieve this aim is the subject of *The Valkyrie*, and we can gain a valuable insight into Wagner's skill as a dramatist if we compare that part of his 'Sketch for a Drama', which treats the subject in only general terms, with the final text. To take one example: in the sketch Wotan does not himself engender the Wälsung race; the twins Siegmund and Sieglinde are only remotely connected with him through the agency of a magic apple he gave their unnamed parents to eat; both have other marriage partners; and their incestuous union is punished by Wotan without any prompting from Fricka. Wotan is simply the remote god, ordering events from afar. In translating these events into practical stage form Wagner did far more, however, than merely simplify personal relationships. He introduced a new element into the drama: love.

It is not only the doomed love of Siegmund and Sieglinde that makes *The Valkyrie* so compelling, but the equally powerful, and dramatically far more complicated, bond between Wotan and his daughter Brünnhilde. Contrasted with this, and giving it yet further dramatic intensity is Wotan's loveless relationship with his wife Fricka. The Wotan of *The Valkyrie* is a very human figure, unlike the ambitious young god of *The Rhinegold* and the worldly-wise Wanderer of *Siegfried*, and it is part of the particular fascination of *The*

Valkyrie that here, for the only time in the whole *Ring*, we see its central character directly depicted in a manner to which we can respond emotionally.

Wotan's conception of love is a narrow one, only incidental to his main purpose of expiating his sin and averting the ending Erda has predicted for the gods. To achieve this result he is still relying on power, and his original aim in fathering both Siegmund and Brünnhilde was to use them as instruments of his own will. The love he has come to feel for them as individual beings is an unforeseen complication, and one that, as *The Valkyrie* shows us, he is unable to control, since he apparently does not understand its implications. His failure leads to the death of Siegmund and the banishment of Brünnhilde.

To emphasise the significance of this new development in his story — the conflict between power and love — Wagner devotes the whole of his first act to an episode which, looked at logically in relation to *The Ring* as a whole, is a minor event: the first encounter (since their childhood separation) between Siegmund and Sieglinde. In this act Wotan plays no part at all: in fact, he is not even mentioned by name, and the lovers connect him neither with their vanished father Wälse nor with the mysterious stranger who plunged a sword into the tree in Hunding's dwelling. (Wotan's unseen presence is of course made known to us, the audience, through the music — to those of us, at any rate, who are familiar with the leitmotifs.)

The vividness with which Wagner has presented the force of love to us in his first act, winning our sympathies for the lovers, and persuading us (if we are susceptible to moral qualms) to forgive them their adultery and incest, puts us firmly on the side of Wotan in his argument with Fricka in the second act. And in order to keep our attention fixed on the main theme, Wagner does not bring in Fricka straight away, but shows us Wotan sporting briefly with his daughter Brünnhilde. Thus, on our first sight of him in this drama, we see him happily enjoying love in the way he tends to see it: as a simple, untroubled form of affectionate companionship. Wotan must once have had feelings of this sort

The Valkyries at Bayreuth in 1896 (Royal Opera House Archives)

8

The Valkyries at Bayreuth, off-stage with their repetiteur Carl Kittl, in 1914 (photo: Sidney Loeb)

for Fricka (to gain whom he after all sacrificed an eye), but all that is now past. Fricka has come to uphold the sanctity of the marriage bond, not of love. Wotan's attempts to point out the difference between these two concepts are all in vain.

The scene, as Wagner originally wrote it, was longer, and more was said about the hollowness of marriage maintained after love is dead. He subsequently shortened the dispute for musical and dramatic reasons, but in his letter to August Röckel of January 25, 1854 he revealed how vital this confrontation between Wotan and his wife was to him in his whole conception of the *Ring*. 'Fear of annihilation is the source of all lovelessness,' he wrote. '... The tight bond that holds them together has its origin in love's involuntary error of prolonging itself beyond the necessity for change ... and exposes both partners to the mutual torment of lovelessness. The subsequent development of the entire drama shows the necessity of recognising ... the eternal newness of reality and of life, and yielding to it.'

Though in his curtailed version he allowed Wotan to lecture Fricka on the importance of acknowledging change, Wagner did not endow his god with the enlightened understanding of love and its opposite, lovelessness, that he himself, as omniscient author, possessed. And deliberately so, for it is precisely on his inability to appreciate the many aspects and potentialities of love that Wotan ('all wrapped up in his scheming,' as Wagner describes him in his letter to Röckel) comes to grief. 'The Spring enticed them to love,' Wotan explains in reply to Fricka's condemnation of Siegmund's and Sieglinde's incestuous union. This suggests that he sees (or claims to see) their act as something rather primitive, a mere capitulation to a physical urge. His defence of it is in any case based less on understanding for the lovers than on the assumption that, in coming together, they are in some way serving his ends.

The essential selfishness of Wotan's feelings for Siegmund and Sieglinde is already clear in the manner in which he has allowed them, his own children, to suffer the miseries of their existence unaided, because it was to his own advantage that Siegmund should be a free agent. In Sieglinde he anyway displays little or no interest. Fricka has no difficulty in overcoming his arguments in their defence: she merely needs to point out the truths that he has been trying to conceal from himself: if Siegmund really is a free agent, she declares, then let him fend for himself against Hunding. The argument is of course unanswerable, and there is nothing Wotan can do but capitulate.

In his subsequent confessions to Brünnhilde Wotan is just enough to place the blame for his dilemma on himself, not on Fricka. All she has done, he bitterly realises, is to shatter his illusions concerning Siegmund's place in his scheme, and he admits: 'With loathing I can find but myself in all my hand has created.' He could of course have come on this self-evident truth without Fricka's aid, but it is a vital element in Wagner's dramatic structure that Brünnhilde should see Fricka departing in triumph, since this provides the motivation for the ensuing dramatic development. Brünnhilde, whose trust in her father was seen at the beginning of the act to be total and unthinking, believes, when he orders her to withdraw her support from Siegmund and allow Hunding to slay him, that Fricka has been responsible for Wotan's change of mind. This gives her the courage to disobey her father, an act of betrayal that would appear arbitrary if we did not know it to be directed, consciously or unconsciously, against Fricka, for whom she has no respect, rather than against Wotan.

Now, as a deeply troubled Brünnhilde comes to the fleeing lovers, Wagner introduces us to that aspect of love that is beyond Wotan's understanding. Its name is compassion, and it is something Brünnhilde too has to learn. She finds it in Siegmund's rejection of the delights of Valhalla since Sieglinde will not be permitted to accompany him there, and in his determination, now that he knows his own death is inevitable, to kill Sieglinde rather than leave her to face life alone. Stirred by his unflinching devotion and stung by his reproach to her for the hardness of her heart, Brünnhilde swiftly forgets her duty to her father: in this instant she is rather the daughter of her mother Erda, whose concern it is to protect the natural order against the ravages of power-hungry gods and dwarfs. It is from Erda, too, that she has acquired her new gift of prophecy: her knowledge that Sieglinde is bearing Siegmund's child in her womb, a fact of which Wotan is seemingly quite unaware. The love that impels her to help the twins and their unborn offspring and to brave her father's wrath is of a different and even higher order than that of the lovers themselves, for it is entirely selfless.

Musically magnificent as this scene between Brünnhilde and Siegmund is, and awe-inspiring the dramatic climax that follows it, there can be no denying that the second act as a whole depends too heavily on its words to match the emotional sweep of the first and third acts. Wagner himself was aware of this. He wrote to Liszt on October 3, 1855: 'I am worried about the weighty second act: it contains two catastrophes, each so significant and so strong that they really provide content enough for two acts. But the one is so dependent on the other and they follow each other so directly that it was quite impossible to separate them. However, if it is ever to be played in the way I wish, it must

Left: Anton von Rooy as Wotan at the Met. in 1898; and right: Milka Ternina as Brünnhilde, a role she sang at Bayreuth for the first time in 1899. (Royal College of Music)

11

Left: Fritz Hübner as Hunding at Covent Garden in 1982; and right: Peter Hofmann as Siegmund and Jeannine Altmeyer as Sieglinde at Covent Garden in 1980 (photos: Reg Wilson)

certainly — if all my intentions are fully understood — produce an effect more shattering than anything that has ever gone before. Things like this are written only for people who have good powers of endurance (so really for nobody!). The fact that the uninitiated or the weak in spirit will complain cannot influence me.'

The secret of appreciating the full force of the second act is, of course, to pay a proper attention to the words — and that goes for the producer, singers and audience alike. The third act, with its exciting opening (the Valkyries) and its profoundly moving close (Wotan's farewell to Brünnhilde) can prove shattering enough even without that aid, but in the central scene between Wotan and Brünnhilde the words are once again of vital importance, for here we see Brünnhilde attempting to explain to her father that new emotion of selfless love that led her to disobey him. It is a vain effort, for Wotan is deeply injured in his pride, too much blinded by rage over the insult to his authority, to listen to her. Love to him is still a selfish delight, indeed, a weakness to be overcome when it threatens power, and Brünnhilde must be punished for giving in to it. Even when she hints that, by disobeying him, she has carried out his ultimate desire — for she has ensured the continuation of the Wälsung race to which he once looked for delivery — he remains unmoved: 'Name not the Wälsungs to me!' Indeed, he is thoroughly incensed that another should claim to be doing something that he himself is unable to do.

In all that he says Wotan reveals the inevitability of his downfall, for he is unable to grasp the nature of that love that alone can bring him salvation. After his argument with Fricka he had bitterly proclaimed his readiness to renounce his power, but now he finds himself unable to do it. The obstinacy of the will is not so easily overcome, and it will even accept the sacrifice of a cherished daughter in order to prevail. His plea that the laws insist on Brünnhilde's punishment for her crime of disobedience is a weak one, since he, as maker of the laws, is only a slave to them to the extent he himself chooses. It is in fact a form of self-exoneration, and as such is a manifestation, not of justice, but of that selfish will that holds Wotan prisoner. Brünnhilde, recognising this, ceases to resist and humbly agrees to accept her punishment.

Yet still she finds the courage to demand a modification of it. Does she foresee — with that gift of prophecy inherited from her mother — that, in asking for her place of sleep to be surrounded by fire, she will ensure that only Siegfried, the fearless Wälsung, will be able to free her? Wagner does not tell us, but Brünnhilde (if she does foresee it) has the wisdom to keep the knowledge from her father and to frame her appeal to him in the only form she is sure he will understand. In begging him not to place her in peril of becoming the slave of an unworthy mortal ('Cast not this shame, this cruel disgrace on me!'), she is appealing directly to his fatherly love — and indirectly to his vanity.

As Wotan departs after the intensely moving farewell scene, we are far too aware of his loneliness and despair to ask ourselves to what extent he is himself responsible for his downfall (that is the word Wagner himself, in his letter to Röckel, applies to Wotan's banishment of Brünnhilde). It is a supreme example of the use of dramatic irony. Wotan's anger at Brünnhilde's flouting of his authority has led him into the very error for which, in the second act, we heard him chiding Fricka: the inability to acknowledge change. He is seemingly unaware that, in having deprived Brünnhilde of her 'godhead' — in other words, her total allegiance to him — he has inevitably surrendered his power to one with a greater understanding of love and its potentialities as a liberating force than his own. From now on Wotan is a 'departed spirit' (Wagner to Röckel again), who can no longer command events, but only accept them as they come.

Gwyneth Jones as Brünnhilde and Donald McIntyre as Wotan at Covent Garden in 1982 (photo: Reg Wilson)

Frida Leider as Brünnhilde and Rudolf Bockelmann as Wotan at Covent Garden in 1934 (Royal Opera House Archives)

Chronology

Principal stages in the composition and production of *The Valkyrie* and *The Ring* cycle.

	Life and Synchronous Events	Prose and Poetical Works	Musical Works
1847	Age: 34		Score of *Lohengrin* completed
1848	Feb., Mar. Revolutions in Paris, Vienna, Berlin	*The Wibelungen: World-history from the Saga*	
		The Nibelungen Myth as sketch for a Drama	
	Nov.	*Siegfried's Death, Jesus of Nazareth*	
1849	May Risings in Dresden. Wagner flees to Paris, then settles in Zurich	*Theatrical Reform, Art & Revolution*, etc.	
1850	Returns to Paris, then Switzerland	*The Art-Work of the Future, Wieland the Smith*, etc.	
1851		*Opera & Drama, A Communication to my Friends*	
	May-June	*Young Siegfried*	
	Autumn	Decision to extend *Siegfried* dramas by depicting the previous events in dramatic form: birth of *The Ring* cycle	
1852	June	*The Valkyrie*	
	Sept-Nov	*The Rhinegold*	
	Nov-Dec	Recasts *Young Siegfried* as *Siegfried*, and *Siegfried's Death* as *Twilight of the Gods*	
1853		*The Ring of the Nibelung* first published, privately	
	Oct.		Working on music of *The Rhinegold*
1854	Jan.		Finishes *The Rhinegold* music
	May		Score of *The Rhinegold* completed. June. Begins music of *The Valkyrie*.
	Autumn Conceives idea of *Tristan*		
	Dec. Reading Schopenhauer		Finishes *The Valkyrie* music
1855	In London & Zurich		*A Faust Overture* Scoring *The Valkyrie*
1856	April		Score of *The Valkyrie* completed

	May	*Die Sieger*: sketch for a Buddhistic drama	Working on music of *Siegfried*
1857	April Settles in Zurich near the Wesendoncks'		
		Aug-Sept. Sketch & poem of *Tristan & Isolde*	July. Completes *Siegfried* Act One & part of Act Two (Then 8 year interval)
			Dec. Completes *Tristan* Act One
1858	Paris, Switzerland		*'Wesendonck' Songs*
1859	Paris		Scoring of *Tristan* completed
1861	Dec.	*The Mastersingers of Nuremberg* poem	
1862	Concert tours: First performances of *The Ride of the Valkyries*		Begins music of *The Mastersingers*
1863	Concert tours	*The Ring* published with a Preface about its stage production	
1864	Ludwig of Bavaria invites him to Munich		
1865	June 10. Munich: First performance of *Tristan*		Resumes composition of *Siegfried*
1866			
1867			Score of *The Mastersingers* completed
1868	June 21. Munich: First performance of *The Mastersingers*		
1869	Sept. 22. Munich: First performance of *The Rhinegold* against Wagner's wishes		*Siegfried* music written *Twilight* music begun
1870	June 26. Munich: First performance of *The Valkyrie* against Wagner's wishes		
1871		*On the production of the Stage Festival-Drama 'The Ring of the Nibelung'*	Score of *Siegfried* completed
1872	Settles in Bayreuth. Foundation of the Festival Theatre	*Epilogue to 'The Ring'*	Finishes *Twilight* music
1873		Completes re-publication of 9 volumes of prose works	Begins score of *Twilight*
1874			Score of *Twilight* completed
1876	Aug. 13, 14, 16 & 17. First complete *Ring* cycle at Bayreuth		

Thérèse Maltan as Brünnhilde, at Bayreuth in the 1890s (Royal College of Music)

Emil Gerhauser at Bayreuth in 1896 (Royal Opera House Archives)

Marie Brema as Fricka at Bayreuth in 1896 (Royal Opera House Archives)

An Introduction to the Music of 'The Valkyrie'

Barry Millington

Every Wagner-lover has a favourite opera: the intense *Tristan and Isolde*, perhaps, or the jovial *Mastersingers*, or the majestic *Parsifal*. But if we are to judge by the criteria of Wagner's own prescription for a new artform, the music drama, in which poetry and music were to be integrated as never before, then we must turn, for the most successful exposition of those principles, to *The Valkyrie*.

The elements of music-drama were laid out in formidable detail in Part Three of Wagner's essay *Opera and Drama* (1851). At the heart of the matter was the creation of a new kind of vocal line, one which was moulded explicitly to carry the nuances of the verse. There was to be no more artificial rhyme, and no more of the regular melodic construction imposed by the straitjacket of conventional four- or eight-bar phrases. *The Rhinegold* was Wagner's first attempt to put his theories into practice and despite its many felicities it is clear that he had not yet found quite the right mix for his ingredients: sometimes a melodic line will perfectly mirror the contours and accents of the verse, but fail to make an emotional impact simply because it is not a sufficiently interesting musical idea; at other times, notably in scenes two and four, there is an occasional relapse into pure recitative, with the appearance in both voice and orchestra of cadential formulas familiar from eighteenth-century opera.

With *The Valkyrie*, however, the synthesis reaches its peak. The work, and especially Act One, is packed with musico-poetic lines that are pregnant with dramatic significance and yet which have the utmost musical appeal. The fact that the second and third acts of *The Valkyrie* begin to move away from the principle of absolute equality of poetry and music may well be connected with Wagner's encounter with Schopenhauer. It was while making his composition sketches for *The Valkyrie* that Wagner first read *The World as Will and Idea* and the philosophy expressed in that book affected him profoundly. Schopenhauer held that music alone was an articulation of what he called the 'will' — the inner world of the imagination. The direct line of communication made it possible for music to express the innermost nature of all life and existence; it was thus more penetrating than and superior to the other forms of art.

Wagner had previously ordained that all the arts must combine equally to form the total work of art (*Gesamtkunstwerk*), but now, in 1854, Schopenhauer's glorification of music provided a philosophical justification for an approach more in accord with Wagner's natural inclination. Even *Opera and Drama* was a step in this direction because the 1849 essay *The Artwork of the Future* had, like *Rhinegold*, given more emphasis to the drama side of the equation: allowance was actually made there for occasional spoken dialogue.

The means by which poetry and music were to be linked in a system of forward- and backward-looking connections was the 'motif of reminiscence'. This was one of the terms by which Wagner referred to what we now call the leitmotif — an expression not used by Wagner himself. However, it did not work in quite the way that he had expected. He had stated in *Opera and Drama* that motifs of reminiscence would only serve to heighten the expressive

17

content of the melodic verse when it approximated the intonation of ordinary speech. When the intensity of melodic verse was greater, the orchestra would fulfil a merely harmonic function. That was the theory, but in practice almost the exact reverse came to apply. Many of the most highly-charged outbursts of the characters in *The Ring* are propelled by motifs of reminiscence, while more low-key passages — such as the beginning of Wotan's Act Two, scene two monologue, *'Als junger Liebe'* ('When youth's delightful pleasures had waned') in *The Valkyrie* — generally elicit fewer, not more, motifs.

Furthermore, Wagner had originally intended that his motifs of reminiscence would be generated by the musico-poetic line as thoughts and emotions were expressed; they would then become the property of the orchestra and any subsequent recurrence in the orchestra alone would be enough to recall the original thought or emotion. Again this did not turn out to be the case: in *Rhinegold* only about half of the motifs originate in the musico-poetic line, in *The Valkyrie* considerably fewer, and in *Tristan* almost none at all.

Commentators frequently complain about Wagner's inconsistency in his use of leitmotif: the Valhalla motif [8], for example, is subsequently applied to Wotan himself, and the ring [6], sword [27] and spear or treaty [9] motifs are sometimes sounded for no apparent reason — that is to say, the object has not been mentioned specifically in the text. But to reduce Wagner's system of motifs to a kind of aural semaphore is drastically to circumscribe his means of expression. While some of the labels that have been attached to motifs are appropriate, others are convenient but ultimately useless. As soon as a leitmotif is given the label 'dejection', 'futility' or 'ambition', the possibility is closed off that the motif is actually representing more than a single psychological impulse. Nor is it reasonable to suppose that an identical dramatic situation can ever re-occur: with the gaining of knowledge and experience, characters' attitudes must be capable of altering with them. As the tetralogy unfolded Wagner found that he needed more and more flexibility to do justice to the immense complex of associations that he was setting up.

In order to increase the available range of sonorities for the delineation of character and mood, and for tone-painting, Wagner expanded his orchestral forces in *The Ring* to an unprecedented scale. He called for quadruple wood-wind (for example, three clarinets and one bass clarinet where *Tannhäuser* and *Lohengrin* had called for only three players) and increased his brass section so that it could divide into four independent families: eight horns, of which four periodically have to switch to provide a family of Wagner tubas; three trumpets and a bass trumpet; three trombones and a contrabass trombone. Trumpets are the obvious instruments to give out Wagner's numerous fanfare-like motifs, such as that of the sword [27], and the latter often appears on the bass trumpet, an instrument that was constructed specially for *The Ring* according to the composer's specifications. Wagner liberated the trombones by making melodic, rather than merely harmonic, demands of them: they are often required to give out the motifs of Wotan's spear [9] and the curse [23].

The celebrated Wagner tubas (again made specially for *The Ring* but this time based on instruments Wagner had seen in the Paris workshop of Adolphe Sax) are actually closer to horns than to tubas: they have horn mouthpieces and are played by the fifth to eighth members of the horn section. Introduced by Wagner in order to furnish a separate brass family (two tenor, two bass, underpinned by a contrabass tuba) of distinctive tone colour and bridging the gap between horns and trombones, their rich, round, solemn sound can be heard in *The Valkyrie* at the entry of Hunding (Act One, scene two) [32] and at

Ludwig Hofmann, a famous Wotan at the Vienna Opera 1935-42

A contemporary cartoon of the effect of Wagner's music on the ear (April 18, 1869)

the beginning of the Annunciation of Death scene (Act Two, scene four) [38]. The intonation of Wagner tubas (also called 'Bayreuth tubas' or in German 'Waldhorntuben') can be troublesome in performance.

Wagner's development of the full potential of the brass department and his mastery in handling the expanded winds and strings — shown in the blending and grouping of instruments and in matters of tonal balance — place him among the most adventurous and most skilled orchestrators of any period. His contemporaries, and not least the cartoonists, were struck above all by the accompanying increase in the volume of sound. But this was purely incidental: Wagner's need was for an orchestral body of sound that could give adequate expression to his complex dramatic conceptions.

Act One

The work opens with a turbulent prelude depicting at once a raging storm and the mental convulsions that are soon to shake the participants in the drama. A tremolo on a single repeated note is kept up by the second violins and violas for 60 bars, while underneath cellos and double basses rampage up and down a series of notes that are clearly intended to recall the motif of the spear [9]: that symbol of Wotan's power and authority is evoked immediately because the whole of this first act is contrived, in a sense, at the instigation of his will. The motif sung by Donner, the god of thunder, at the end of *Rhinegold* to the words *'Heda! Hedo!'* [26], rings out on the brass, first on the Wagner tubas. It is surely no accident that despite the different harmonic context it begins in B flat, precisely as in *Rhinegold*; however, it is winched up sequentially through a series of modulations until the tension breaks in a thunderclap, after which the storm begins to subside. As Siegmund enters the forest dwelling, a cello takes up the spear motif but turns its end accommodatingly back on itself [28];

we do not yet know what this signifies, but may suppose that an alternative to sheer, naked power is being proposed. Sieglinde enters, and as she bends over his sleeping figure that idea is taken up again and now combined with a motif [29] expressive of Sieglinde's tenderness. The two melodic ideas are worked together and reach a small climax; when Sieglinde returns with water for him, [28] opens out into what we can identify as a fully-fledged love theme, the music as yet anticipating events on the stage. This new theme [30] is a derivation of the second part of that associated with Freia [11b], heard in *Rhinegold* when she enters pursued by the giants. Since Hans von Wolzogen compiled the first thematic guide, it has been identified with the notion of flight. Yet, as Deryck Cooke conclusively showed in his sadly unfinished study of *The Ring**, the theme is a central love theme in the work. Originally confined to Siegmund and Sieglinde, it later undergoes considerable development in connection with other characters. Furthermore, it is based on a pattern of notes that recurs in motifs associated with love in other Wagner operas, for instance in the Prize Song in *The Mastersingers*.

Sieglinde fetches a horn of mead for Siegmund and [29] spread its wings in a glorious A major passage, the bassoons, horns and clarinets lending a bloom to the strings. The two halves of [30] are heard in reverse order as the pair gaze at each other in unspoken affirmation of love. The minor triad [31] evokes the ill luck which dogs Siegmund. This Wälsung motif is combined with [29] as he decides to stay and await his fate.

In scene two, Hunding's entry is announced by the Wagner tubas with [32], a sharp, abrupt motif that contrasts with the pliant ones of Siegmund and Sieglinde. Siegmund recounts his story and Hunding eventually identifies him as his enemy. The motif of the Wälsungs, the race of Siegmund and Sieglinde, is heard, the absence of upper strings giving it a dark colouring.

Scene three finds Siegmund left alone; he calls on his father who had promised him a weapon in time of need: *'Wälse! Wälse!'* The shifts of pace leading to this climactic outburst are notable; reflective passages alternate with heroic as the sense of the words is projected explicitly through the vocal line and its accompaniment. Momentum is quickly built up in an eight-bar period, *'Zu der mich nun Sehnsucht zieht'* (lit. Yearning now draws me to her), which is expanded by a bar deliberately to increase the tension. The *Wälse!* cries themselves, so often regarded by singers and listeners alike as a test of virility, are simply the octave leap of the sword motif [27b] without the tail-piece. They launch Siegmund on a heart-warming soliloquy, richly orchestrated, the rippling harp arpeggios mirroring the gleaming of the sword in the ash tree.

Sieglinde enters and tells Siegmund the story of how an old man dressed in grey thrust the sword in the tree at the wedding ceremony of Sieglinde and Hunding. This is one of the finest of the many fine examples of musico-poetic synthesis that abound in this act. The sounding of the Valhalla motif [8] by horns and bassoons, announcing the real identity of the stranger at the wedding, is one of the classic uses of leitmotif to commentate on the action. But we should also notice the low-lying vocal line depicting the Wanderer's low-brimmed hat, the shape of the melodic line portraying the flash of his eye and then its 'threatening glance', the falling chromatic intervals for his lingering look of yearning, the expressive appoggiatura on *'Tränen'* ('tears'), and the final rise to a top G for the physical act of implanting the sword in the tree. The duet gets under way (Wagner still true to his principles at this point

* *I Saw the World End* (Oxford, 1979)

Frederick Dalberg as Hunding and Maria Olczewska as Fricka (Royal Opera House Archives)

does not allow the couple to sing together) but there is a temporary slackening of pace for Siegmund's celebrated *'Winterstürme wichen dem Wonnemond'* ('Winter storms have vanished at Spring's command'). This has become famous as a tenor song extracted from its context and performed separately. Indeed it begins like a conventional operatic aria: the A section is twenty bars in length, and a contrasting key appears to introduce a B section, but after only nine bars the second part of [30] bursts in and we are swept off in a different direction. Incomplete and hybrid structures of this kind are absolutely typical in Wagner's music dramas; recognizable forms are continually evolving into something different.

For the remainder of the act, an ecstatic declaration of mutual love, we may choose to sit back and not worry unduly about the motifs flitting past, though more careful study of the musico-poetic line and the harmonic structure certainly repays itself. It is necessary to mention just one point that has been the cause of much agonising. As Siegmund pulls the sword out of the tree, he intones the motif [7] often known, after its appearance in *The Rhinegold*, as the renunciation of love. What is the meaning of this? Siegmund is clearly doing anything but renouncing love. Is this a serious flaw in Wagner's system? Complicated and contorted explanations have been offered, but in essence the matter is simple. The love that has been awakened in Siegmund seems at this juncture to be what is needed to restore a world order based on compassion rather than the wielding of power. The sword presents him with the means to bring this restoration about. Nothing could be more relevant at this point than the recollection of Alberich's sacrifice of love in order to gain power. Siegmund may be unaware of the existence of Alberich but we, the audience, are allowed a timely reminder of the struggle of the opposing forces of love and power that underpins the drama.

Act Two

The music of the prelude, heard before the curtain rises on Wotan and his Valkyrie daughter Brünnhilde (both fully armed), anticipates the Ride of the Valkyries in the Third Act. Its enormous vitality is generated by the dotted rhythms in 9/8 time [34], and augmented fifths — a favourite chord of Wagner's — heighten the tension. A variant of the sword motif [27] is given out by the trumpet and bass trumpet *fortissimo* and the motif first associated with Freia [11b] is also prominent. Brünnhilde's joyful warcry *'Hojotoho!'* [35] soon takes her up to top Bs and Cs, but she makes herself scarce as Fricka arrives in her ram-drawn chariot for an extended confrontation with Wotan — a magnificent piece of music drama. Fricka's complaint is that the sibling lovers have violated the marriage vows of which she is the guardian. Wotan's tender, if slightly disingenuous, reply that love was responsible evokes [30b]. Fricka continues to protest and embarks on an arioso passage in the unusual key of G sharp minor to make her point.

This passage, which at first glance appears to be a reversion to an old-style form, in fact displays considerable subtlety in its variety of pace and irregular phrase-lengths. Moreover, it is an example of a characteristic feature of Wagner's mature style: the occasional removal, as it were, onto a plateau where the melodic material is new and distinctive, and takes over momentarily from the stock of leitmotifs. Other examples are to be found at the end of *Siegfried* with Brünnhilde's *'Ewig war ich'* ('Ever was I'), which uses the *Siegfried Idyll* music, and in Act Two of *Tristan and Isolde* at *'O sink' hernieder'* as the lovers settle down on the flowery bank.

In the ensuing exchanges between Fricka and Wotan, Fricka devastatingly exposes the flaw in the guilty god's argument: Siegmund is not able to act as a free hero so long as he is protected by Wotan. As Wotan thrashes about in despair, much use is made of [36], a motif which Ernest Newman labelled simply 'Dejection', but whose contorted melodic shape and kinship to the spear motif [9] suggest something more specific: the frustration of Wotan's will. Fricka extracts from Wotan an oath that he will no longer protect his son.

In scene two Wotan continues to writhe in mental agony [36] and Brünnhilde reappears to receive the full brunt of his outburst of grief and frustration: *'O heilige Schmach!'* ('O infinite shame!'). A powerful climax is generated by the dissonant piling up of motifs, initiated by the new [9b]. This is primarily an inversion of [36] but is also related to Wotan's authority [9]; it is followed immediately by a reminder of the curse on the ring [23]. The notes to which Wotan sings *'Endloser Grimm! Ewiger Gram!'* ('Endless remorse! Grief evermore!') are in fact [30a], a poignant indication that it is lack of love that is the cause of his troubles.

The following encounter between Wotan and Brünnhilde outstrips even the previous scene for dramatic excitement. Those unsympathetic to Wagner's method of myth compression and dramatisation have often pointed to this scene as an example of superfluous recapitulation caused by the fact that Wagner wrote the texts of the tetralogy in the reverse order of the events

Lauritz Melchior as Siegmund (Royal Opera House Archives)

Lotte Lehmann as Sieglinde (Rubini Records)

of the drama. But such a view ignores the vital point that these narratives invariably afford insights into the narrator and that the perspective in which they are related is always illuminating. In this case, Wotan is persuaded to lay bare his soul to his favourite daughter and her sympathy encourages him to articulate and come to terms with his dilemma. Wotan begins the exchange by confessing how he attempted to fill the vacuum of lovelessness in his life by acquiring power. His hushed reliving of the story, *'Als junger Liebe'*, is the closest thing in the whole work to pure recitative, but it is by no means oblivious to the *Opera and Drama* principles of word-setting and in any case it acquires a special aura of suspense from the accompaniment — double basses alone, *pianissimo*. The characteristic motifs appear as Wotan recalls the theft of the gold, the building of Valhalla, the ring. [24] and [36] are prominent, both individually and in conjunction [36b]. The curse [23] and the sword [27] drive the monologue to a tremendous climax: Wotan looks for only one thing — *'das Ende'* ('the ending'). His first utterance of the fearful word is followed by a stunned silence, the second by the motif of Erda [24], whose prophecy Wotan now understands. Brünnhilde, who hitherto has said little, suggests that she might disobey Wotan and protect Siegmund in accordance with his true wishes; this psychologically painful situation provokes an emphatic re-

23

Ann Howard as Fricka at ENO in 1975 (photo: John Garner)

Yvonne Minton as Fricka at Covent Garden in 1982 (photo: Reg Wilson)

statement, on bassoons, horns, cellos and basses, of [9] and Wotan storms off asserting his authority.

Siegmund and Sieglinde enter in haste (scene three), the orchestra making much of [11b]; clearly this is one of the passages that caused it to be misnamed the 'flight' motif. We hear various motifs associated with the Wälsungs and their love but the music becomes even more agitated as Sieglinde, terror-struck, begins to hallucinate. She swoons and Siegmund is still holding her when Brünnhilde reappears for the fourth scene. Yet another remarkable creation, the Annunciation of Death is often regarded as the focal centre of the whole tetralogy, the scene on which the drama turns. It opens with the solemn intoning, on the Wagner tubas, of [38], whose interrogatory melodic shape and dominant 7th have generally earned it a label such as 'destiny' or 'fate'. It is heard throughout the scene, as is [37], whose close is the same as [38]. Three distinct brass groupings are used to conjure a mood of quiet, noble heroism: Wagner tubas, trumpets and trombones, horns with bassoons. Deeply impressed by Siegmund's resolution and love for Sieglinde, Brünnhilde eventually promises him her protection, which, in the fifth and final scene she gives him — but to no avail: Wotan's power is stronger.

Act Three

Those whose only experience of Wagner has been *The Ride of the Valkyries* may be forgiven an attitude of defensive caution. Of all the purple passages that have been torn from their context and over-exposed, this must be the least subtle. And yet there is much to recommend it: the piece has an immense sense of exultation and verve which, in the theatre, when it is sung and staged, can be a thrilling experience. As for the scoring, it illustrates a characteristic and unmistakable mannerism of Wagner: a brass theme in unison cutting across a dense texture, in this case of thrilling, antiphonal woodwind and swirling string arpeggios. In rehearsal, Wagner was particularly concerned that the main accent of the brass theme should fall on the first beat, rather than on the second group of three, since the E already receives emphasis on account of its higher pitch [34].

As Wotan approaches, Brünnhilde urges Sieglinde to flee for safety; what persuades the distraught woman is the news that she is carrying a Wälsung in her womb. This announcement is made with [39], an expansive theme whose heroic ring prompts Sieglinde to react with the work's most enraptured melodic inspiration [40]. It returns at the end of *Twilight of the Gods* to accompany Brünnhilde's expiatory act of self-immolation; it is, in fact, the last motif heard in *The Ring*. Wagner referred to it as 'the glorification of Brünnhilde'.

Wotan arrives, the pleas of Brünnhilde's Valkyrie sisters are ignored, and Wotan and Brünnhilde remain alone. She asks whether by contravening his orders she was not in fact carrying out his inward wishes; she uses a theme derived from that of the spear [9], the symbol of Wotan's authority, but turns,

Kirsten Flagstad (Brünnhilde) and Hans Hotter (Wotan) at Covent Garden in 1948 (photo: Roger Wood)

Norman Bailey in the ENO production designed by Ralph Koltai (photo: John Garner)

by octave displacement, its severity into an eloquent melody:

She recalls the experience of the Annunciation of Death [37, 38], which had persuaded her to shield Siegmund, and now [41], which like the new melody is derived from [9], blossoms forth in a transported E major: Brünnhilde's compassionate love thus stands opposed to Wotan's tyrannical wielding of power, but also, in motivic terms, grows organically out of it.

Throughout the unfolding of this scene more and more motifs are recalled from the past as emotionally charged memories are brought to the surface. Careful listening to the thematic constitution of this scene, coupled with a close reading of the text, pays dividends. Two new motifs remain to be mentioned: [42], whose sinking semitonal melodic line and trance-like mediant progressions are a perfect evocation of the 'magic sleep'; and [43], which is heard in an ominous minor key as Brünnhilde dreads being woken from her long sleep by an unworthy coward, but which in its major form acquires a luminous, hypnotic quality in the closing pages of the score.

The last part of this scene is a succession of carefully controlled climaxes, none of which is more affecting than that following Wotan's grief-stricken farewells to Brünnhilde (*'Leb'wohl!'*). Wagner's skill in pacing the action over such vast expanses, his sure handling of character and psychology, and not least his transformation of the genre from a mere assemblage of melodies into vibrant drama, combining deeply felt music and poetry: these are qualities that have given *The Valkyrie* a justified reputation as one of Wagner's most impressive, as well as one of his most approachable, achievements.

New Myths for Old

George Gillespie

Wagner clearly stated his views on the treatment of myth in *Opera and Drama* (1851): 'The incomparable thing about myth is that it is true for all time, and its content, however closely compressed, is inexhaustible throughout the ages. The only task of the poet is to expound it.'[1] He felt justified, therefore, in reshaping old traditions for the modern world; furthermore, he claimed to be doing what the Greek dramatists had done: 'Tragedy is nothing else but the artistic completion of myth itself, while myth is the poem of a view of life held in common.' His dramatic method is, indeed, not unlike that of Aeschylus, and the redeeming love of Brünnhilde has been compared sometimes to that of Antigone in Sophocles's play, i.e. human love versus state oppression. Wagner, on the other hand, expounds his own extremely personal view of the world through his myth-creation from sources with very different values.

His process of composition reflects his inspiration of linking the story of Siegfried with the activities of the immortals, in which he was probably influenced by the examples of Homer and Virgil. His conception of *The Ring* goes back to the year 1848, when he attempted to link the historical Wibelungs (Ghibellines) with the legendary Nibelungs in *Die Wibelungen*: Siegfried is conceived as a sun-god and the treasure as the embodiment of power. He immediately followed this with *Der Nibelungen-Mythus* — 'as sketch for a Drama' — the kernel of the whole story. By the end of 1852, he had revised the Grand Heroic Opera he had first conceived in 1848 as *Siegfrieds Tod* (*Siegfried's Death*) as the final drama of the tetralogy, *Twilight of the Gods*, and the cycle texts were complete. The pessimistic outcome, already dimly conceived by the poet, was only made clear to him after reading Schopenhauer — in the original version a ray of hope was suggested in that Brünnhilde leads the 'free' hero, Siegfried, to Valhalla.

The early nineteenth-century interpretations of German and Scandinavian traditions concerning Siegfried and the Nibelungen had, in fact, concentrated on their mythical aspects; the brothers Grimm, in particular, were occupied in rescuing the fragmentary evidence of Germanic mythology and heroic tradition from oblivion — a search for national reassurance in material going back, as they felt, to the origins of the German people. With this mythical aspect in mind, namely the struggle between good and evil, light and darkness, between the gods and the Nibelungen, Wagner steeped himself in the mythology of the German and Scandinavian Middle Ages.

In reply to an enquiry made in 1856 Wagner gave the following impressive list of his sources: *Das Nibelungenlied*, a strophic epic composed in Austria *c.* 1200; Karl Lachmann's commentary on it (1836); *Das deutsche Heldenbuch* (1827), a collection of late medieval German heroic epics; the *Poetic Edda*, a collection of lays concerning gods and heroes in alliterative verse made in Iceland *c.* 1250; two works by the great Icelandic scholar and statesman, Snorri Sturluson (†1241), the *Prose Edda*, a compilation of mythological lore, and the *Heimskringla*, in which Óđin (Wagner's Wotan), with the attributes both of a god and of a mortal ruler, is placed at the head of the genealogy of the Kings of Norway; the Þiðriks saga, a compilation of heroic tales, based on German sources made in Norway *c.* 1260, and the *Völsunga saga*, a

27

consecutive account of the ancestry, life, and death of Sigurd (Wagner's Siegfried), composed in Iceland or Norway *c.* 1260. He also had recourse to two outstanding works of scholarship: Wilhelm Grimm's *Die deutsche Heldensage* (1829), in which are assembled all important sources of knowledge about the heroic past. The work that influenced him most, perhaps, was Jacob Grimm's monumental compilation of everything that could be found in literature and folk memory to do with the ancient gods and myths of the Germanic peoples, *Deutsche Mythologie* (1835, 2nd ed. 1844).[2]

From Karl Simrock's sensitive translations of the Icelandic lays he derived his alliterative verse form, which is ideally suited to musical accompaniment, since such lays were composed for recitation and were probably accompanied by stringed instruments; he does not follow the ancient form slavishly, but uses the alliteration and terse verbal formulations to drive home his meaning; as in the lays, the words are of immense importance in *The Ring*. Wagner also uses some stylistic devices of heroic poetry, such as the foreshadowing of coming events and the use of symbols to link past, present, and future — the ring and the sword are the more obvious examples; to provide information he uses the question-and-answer technique he would have found in the *Poetic* and *Prose Eddas*.

The *Nibelungenlied*[3] tells the story of Siegfried's death and the revenge taken by his widow on his murderers, but its author restricts supernatural matters to a bare minimum. Its author, like Wagner, was concerned to demonstrate the dire result of ruthless power politics and the disregard of human values; in this connection, one small episode may well have impressed Wagner: when Hagen, after Siegfried's murder, sinks the treasure in the Rhine, the narrator states:

> The most perfect golden wand lay among it. He who realised that would have been able to be the master of every man in the whole world.

In his Scandinavian sources the ring included with the treasure only has the power to increase it. For his mythological background Wagner turned elsewhere, but he took the name of Alberich from the *Nibelungenlied*, where he is the dwarf-guardian of the treasure, and made him the father of Hagen on a hint from the Þiðriks saga, where Hagen is indeed the son of an elf; furthermore, he lets Alberich replace Andvari, the original dwarf-owner of the treasure and ring seized by the gods in the Scandinavian myth concerning the origin of the hoard won by Sigurd from the dragon. Using another myth from the Eddaic sources, Wagner links the seizure of the treasure with the payment of the giants for building Valhalla. By these brilliant inventions he aligns Siegfried's murder by Hagen with the conflict between Wotan and Alberich for the ring of power, and Siegfried's death preludes the destruction of the gods, just as the death of the youthful Baldr does in Scandinavian mythology.

The conflict between the gods and the Nibelungen, that is between authority and the treasure-seeking and industrious dwarfs, symbolises the ruthless struggle for power in a society without love. In this sense *The Valkyrie* is the key drama of *The Ring*, for it demonstrates in human terms the endangered yet persistent nature of love in such a society. The main source for *The Valkyrie* is the *Völsunga saga*, of which the following is a summary of chapters 1-12:

> Völsung, the grandson of Óðin, has ten sons and a daughter Signý, the twin sister of the eldest son, Sigmund. When Signý is married against her will to Siggeir, a one-eyed man in a cape and low hood (i.e. Óðin)

appears at the marriage feast and plunges a sword into the trunk of the tree growing in the middle of the hall,[4] as a gift for the man who can withdraw it. Sigmund alone can do so, and he refuses to sell it to Siggeir, who departs with his wife in an evil mood.

In spite of Signý's warning of treachery, Völsung accepts Siggeir's invitation to a feast; in the ensuing conflict Völsung is killed and his ten sons set in stocks; nine of them are devoured by Siggeir's mother in wolf-shape; Sigmund kills her and lives in an underground retreat in the forest. Signý sends her two sons to him, but urges him to kill them when they proved too faint-hearted for the task of avenging the deaths of Völsung and his sons. She then exchanges shapes with a sorceress and sleeps three nights with her brother Sigmund, by whom she bears a son, Sinfjötli, who proves impervious to pain. Sigmund and Sinfjötli put on wolfskins, live as werewolves in the forest and kill many men. When they finally enter Siggeir's dwelling in order to exact vengeance, they are discovered by two other sons of Signý, and she has them killed by Sigmund and Sinfjötli. Father and son are captured by Siggeir's men and buried under a great stone slab; Signý smuggles Sigmund's sword in to them, and they saw their way out with it. Signý now reveals to Sigmund that Sinfjötli is their son, which accounts for his prowess. She then returns to the hall, which her brother and son have set on fire, to perish with her husband.

Sigmund returns to his kingdom and marries Borghild, by whom he has a son named Helgi. Helgi kills a king named Hunding. After that fight, he meets the valkyrie Sigrún, who is to be married against her will to Hoddbrodd. Helgi defeats and kills Hoddbrodd; Sigrún with eight other valkyries appears over the battlefield. Helgi marries Sigrún and takes over Hoddbrodd's kingdom.

Meanwhile, Borghild has poisoned Sinfjötli for killing her brother in a feud about a woman, and Sigmund banishes her. He now marries Hjördis, whose former suitor, the son of Hunding, invades his realm. During the battle a one-eyed man in a cape and low hood (Ódin again) places his spear before Sigmund and breaks his sword with it. Sigmund is mortally wounded. On the battlefield he gives Hjördis the sword-fragments, which will be forged into the sword Gram for their future son. Hjördis flees to Denmark, where her son Sigurd is born.

As if by the deft shake of a kaleidoscope, Wagner has produced from this string of episodes a well-motivated drama, in which every event interlocks with the grand design of *The Ring*, namely to contrast the power of human love with the tyranny of traditional authority and the lust for power. The ring of power remains the focal point in *The Valkyrie*: even though Wotan has begotten Brünnhilde and her eight sister valkyries[5], the former by the seeress, Erda,[6] to recruit fallen heroes for the defence of Valhalla, he cannot feel secure till the ring has been recovered. For this purpose he has begotten, under the name of Wälse, the twins Siegmund and Sieglinde by a mortal woman — here Wagner has simplified Siegmund's geneaology by making Wotan his father.[7] Siegmund is to be the 'free' hero who can win back the ring, since Wotan, as the upholder of law, cannot break his agreement with the giants, to whom he handed over the ring and treasure in payment for building Valhalla; but he knows that Alberich has a son by a mortal woman and intends, too, to recover the ring. We learn all this from Wotan's heart-searching revelations to Brünnhilde (Act Two, scene two).

For the action proper of *The Valkyrie*, the *Völsunga saga* provides the material for the first two acts, while Wagner provides the motivation. He has combined the cold-blooded Signý with the pathetic Hjördís to produce Siegmund's bride and sister and given her the name of Siegfried's mother in the *Nibelungenlied*, Sieglinde. By eliminating Sinfjötli he has made Siegfried the offspring of their incestuous union: their incest is made to appear, not a matter of convenience as in the *Völsunga saga*, but the passionate challenge of human love to the tyranny of traditional social rules; their future son Siegfried, then, must inherit two qualities necessary to the 'free' hero: fearlessness in the face of power and a disinterested human warmth; these are demonstrated gloriously in *Siegfried* and tragically in *Twilight of the Gods*.

In Act One, as Siegmund's identity is revealed through back-narration, so the sword, the symbol of defiance, gradually assumes greater importance. Siegmund at first conceals his identity through play on the significance of names: because of his experiences he maintains that his name can never be 'Friedmund' ('guardian of peace'), a play on his real name ('guardian of victory'), nor 'Frohwalt' ('purveyor of joy'), and he finally settles for 'Wehwalt' ('purveyor of woe').[8] While explaining this self-naming by describing his life as an outlaw with his father, he adds to the mystification by referring to his father as 'Wolfe' and himself as 'Wölfing' ('Wolf' and 'Son of Wolf') — here Wagner has transferred the werewolf existence of Sigmund and Sinfjötli (see above) to Wotan (alias Wälse) and Siegmund; the last he saw of his father was his cast-off wolfskin,[9] after the Wälsung homestead had been burnt and his mother killed by the Neidings. Siegmund's attempt to save a woman from a forced marriage (see Helgi's rescue of Sigrún above) has ended in the death of the woman, the slaughter of her kin, and the shattering of his spear and sword. Hunding,[10] under whose roof Siegmund has taken refuge and whose kin have also been slaughtered in that fight, now regards the stranger as his foe and challenges the weaponless man to combat the next day. Full recognition of Siegmund is reserved for his sister Sieglinde, and it coincides with the discovery of the sword. She tells of her abduction by the Neidings and of how they handed her over to Hunding, whom she was forced to marry.[11] Siegmund recalls his father's promise of a 'sword in need', and Sieglinde tells of the grey-clad man with a hat covering one eye who plunged a sword into the house-tree at her wedding feast. Wagner has skilfully reserved the triumphant withdrawal of the sword Notung (German 'Not', 'need') by Siegmund to the end of Act One, when brother and sister realise their kinship and fall into each other's arms. The final words *'Braut und Schwester bist du dem Bruder* — *so blühe denn, Wälsungenblut'* ('Bride and sister be to your brother, the blood of the Walsungs shall flourish!') are a considerable improvement on Signý's matter-of-fact reference to Sinfjötli: 'His immense vigour comes from being King Völsung's grandson on his father's as well as his mother's side.'[12]

The intervention of Odin brings Sigmund's career to an end in the *Völsunga saga*. In Acts Two and Three Wagner has combined it with the account of her enchanted sleep, which Brynhild gives to Sigurd at their first meeting on the mountain top (*Völsunga saga*, ch. 21):

Brynhild told how two kings had been fighting. One was called Hjálmgunnar — he was old and a fine warrior, and Óðin had promised him the victory; and the other was called Agnar.

'In the battle I struck down Hjálmgunnar, and in retaliation Óðin pricked me with the sleep thorn, said that I should never again win a

30

victory, and that I was to marry. And in return I made a solemn vow to marry no one who knew the meaning of fear.'

Wagner has replaced Hjálmgunnar and Agnar by Hunding and Siegmund, making Brünnhilde's disobedience the crux of the drama. Initially Wotan is on the side of his incestuous children when he orders Brünnhilde to kill Hunding in the impending fight (Act Two, scene one). Wotan's change of mind after Fricka's intervention provides a motive for Brünnhilde's opposition to Wotan's counter-order (scene two), which is reinforced by her comprehension of the nature of human love, when Siegmund rejects her summons to Valhalla if Sieglinde cannot go with him: this rejection of divine authority without love and Brünnhilde's awakening compassion provide the central scene in *The Valkyrie* (scene four), and indeed of *The Ring*. Wagner has then fused the death of Sigmund and Hjördis's preservation of the sword-fragments with Brynhild's disobedience to create the dramatic climax, when Brünnhilde attempts to shield Siegmund, but is foiled by the sudden appearance of Wotan, who breaks Siegmund's sword with his spear, so that Hunding is able to kill him. He then scornfully despatches Hunding, as Brünnhilde rides off with the swooning Sieglinde and the sword-fragments (scene five).

Fricka's intervention is another invention of Wagner.[13] From Grimm's *Mythologie* Wagner would have known of Fricka (Old Norse Frigg) as the presiding deity over hearth and home and the upholder of marriage; in the same source he could read how Wodan, according to an eighth-century account, was tricked by his wife into granting victory to the Langobards; from the *Grimnismál* (*Lay of Grimnir*) in the *Poetic Edda* he could learn how Frigg persuades Ódin to abandon one of his protégés. In scene two, therefore, Wotan explains at length the reversal of his decision to Brünnhilde and describes his predicament; he declares despairingly that he can only create puppets: 'This free one whom I have longed for, / this free one can never be found; / for the

Rita Gorr as Fricka and Hans Hotter as Wotan at Covent Garden in 1961 (photo: Anthony Crickmay)

31

free man must be self-created; my hand can only shape slaves!' At this point he gloomily looks forward to the end, when he can hand over his creation to a truly free hero — a foreshadowing of events in *Siegfried* and *Twilight of the Gods*. Brünnhilde is the link between the immortals and humanity, for the hopeless situation of the lovers, demonstrated by Sieglinde's pathetic flight from Siegmund in shame (scene three), is followed by Brünnhilde's change of heart when Siegmund defies the god's decision to summon him to Valhalla (scene four) — both scenes are pure Wagnerian inventions, presenting the predicament of human love in a world of power.

The opening of Act Three provides a contrast with the raucous behaviour of her eight sister valkyries, whose names, apart from that of Siegrune (Old Norse Sigrún), Wagner has invented, though, as in the story of Helgi and Sigrún, he has kept to the traditional number of nine.[14] He has added further 'local colour' to the scene by giving names culled from heroic tradition to the warriors carried by the valkyries across their saddles,[15] and by letting Brünnhilde refer to the furiously pursuing Wotan as 'Der wilde Jäger, / der wütend mich jagt' ('The Wild Huntsman, who pursues me in fury') — in German folk belief the 'Wild Huntsman' led a throng of damned souls, sometimes called 'das wütende Heer' ('the furious host'), which Grimm relates to the cult of Wodan as the god of war. Before Wotan's 'furious' arrival Brünnhilde directs Sieglinde to the forest haunted by the dragon Fafner and gives her the sword-fragments to be forged for her future son. Brünnhilde gives him the name 'Siegfried', interpreting it as 'erfreu sich des Siegs!' ('rejoice in victory!').[16]

In scene two the indignant Wotan condemns Brünnhilde to sleep on the mountain top and marry the first man to wake her; he rejects her excuse that she had acted in defence of love and in accordance with his initial command before Fricka's intervention; he tells her she can henceforth follow this soft-hearted love, while he must, however reluctantly, preserve his authority based on law (scene three). As in the *Völsunga saga*, ch. 21, he grants her request that only a man without fear shall find her on the mountain top. He kisses her eyes, and she falls asleep; then he closes her helmet.[17] The final climax comes when he calls on Loge to surround 'Brünnhildes Fels' (Brünnhilde's Rock')[18] with fire — the involvement of Loge is another invention of Wagner.[19] Wotan's final words point forward to Siegfried's defiance of the god and his winning of Brünnhilde by passing through the wall of flame in *Siegfried*: 'Wer meines Speeres Spitze fürchtet, / durchschreite das Feuer nie!' ('Let the man who fears my spear-point / never pass through the fire'). In contrast to the finale of *The Rhinegold*, where Valhalla, the symbol of authority and power, glows in the evening sun, love, ready to be awakened, lies behind the wall of flame in the form of the sleeping Brünnhilde.

It has been necessary to analyse the text of *The Valkyrie* in some detail because of the way Wagner has closely integrated his own creation with the sources of his material: he has done this structurally through the motivation of the action of the drama by transforming episodic epic and lyric forms for the theatre. He has achieved a variety of contrasting scenes: Siegmund and Sieglinde's love and recognition in adversity (Act One); the confrontations between Fricka and Wotan, and Wotan and Brünnhilde, resulting in Siegmund's judicial murder (Act Two); the violence of the valkyries and Wotan's fury, Wotan's reflective confession to Brünnhilde, and his touching farewell to her (Act Three). The dramatic moments at the end of each act, all stem from the *Völsunga saga* and exemplify Wagner's blending of the two separate plots: the withdrawal of the sword, from Sigmund's story (Act One);

his death coinciding with the valkyrie's disobedience (Act Two) and the calling up of fire to surround the sleeping valkyrie, from Brynhild's story (Act Three).

From a close knowledge of his sources Wagner was able to manipulate his material for his own purposes and yet produce solutions compatible with the mythical and heroic contexts in which his drama is set. In the sagas the heroic figures rarely show compassion, and passionate love frequently engenders feuding, revenge, and murder; but Wagner has imbued his characters with humane qualities without apparent incongruity. Only in the violent scenes where the valkyries and the raging Wotan appear does he introduce somewhat superficial Germanic 'local colour' from a variety of sources.

His greatest creation is the character of Brünnhilde from the brief episode of the awakening of the valkyrie (*Völsunga saga*, ch. 21); by linking her with the fortunes of Siegmund (*Völsunga saga*, chs 1-12), she becomes involved with humanity — her 'punishment' is to cease being immortal and to experience the human feeling of love. In *The Valkyrie* her 'awakening' is a spiritual one, an awakening to the need for love in the ordering of the affairs of the world. She is so important because she indicates the possibility of bridging the gap between this human need and an authority that rules the world by power alone; this possibility may be realised by a 'free' hero, but is left in abeyance, for elucidation in *Siegfried*.

Amalie Materna, the first Brünnhilde in 'The Ring' and Kundry in 'Parsifal' at Bayreuth.

Notes

[1] cit. Derek Cooke, *I Saw the World End*, Oxford 1979, p. 87.
[2] Translated by J.S. Stallybrass, *Teutonic Mythology*, London 1883-8. An excellent account of the Scandinavian mythology is H.R. Ellis Davidson's *Gods and Myths of Northern Europe*, Penguin Books 1964.
[3] Translated into English by A.T. Hatto, Penguin Books 1965.
[4] A terrestrial equivalent of the World Tree, Yggdrasill, the centre of the universe in Scandinavian mythology.
[5] There is no evidence in the mythology that Óðin or Wodan is the father of the valkyries, though Grimm, going on Óðin's by-name Óski and the occasional term óskmey, 'wish-maiden', for valkyrie assumes just this.
[6] Wagner accepts Grimm's postulated earth-goddess, whose name he assumed from the Old High German erda, 'earth', and gave her the characteristics of the Scandinavian völva, 'wise woman', whom Óðin calls up from the dead in the Eddic lay *Völuspà* (*The Sybil's Prophecy*). Óðin does marry an earth-goddess named Iörd.
[7] In this Wagner follows the evidence of the eighth-century Old English *Beowulf*, where Sigemund's father is named Wæls — his patronymic is Wælsung —, and concurs with recent scholarship in assuming that Wæls is none other than Wöden.
[8] The name-component -walt is related to German walten, 'to rule, be in charge of' while -mund indicates guardianship.
[9] 'Wolf' can signify 'exile' or 'outlaw'. The transformation into a wolf was thought to be achieved by wearing a wolfskin.
[10] Wagner has given Sieglinde's husband the name of the shadowy figure of Hunding and the sinister character of Siggeir, and attributed to him the practice of hunting his foes with dogs (German Hunde).
[11] Such an abduction by vikings would have been known to Wagner from Simrock's translation of *Kudrun* (1843), a thirteenth-century German epic, in which the heroine endures privation rather than marry her abductor. The Neidings derive their name from the Old Norse nîðingr, 'vicious, malicious person'.
[12] Quotations are from R.G. Finch, *The Saga of the Volsungs*, London 1965.
[13] Her arrival on a chariot drawn by two rams does not occur in the mythology, though other deities are drawn by various beasts. Grimm only mentions rams in connection with the Greek god Hermes.
[14] The concept of the valkyrie, 'chooser of the slain', may well go back to the priestesses of ancient Germanic ritual, who cast spells to protect the warriors and were involved in the sacrifice of prisoners to the war-god, Óðin-Wodan. Apart from Siegrune ('victory-spell'), which is a valkyrie name in his sources, Wagner has given his valkyries women's names containing components suggesting war: Gerhilde ('spear-conflict'), Orthilde ('spear-point — dragon'), Waltraute ('slaughter — devoted'), Helmwige ('helmet — battle'), Grimgerde ('grim-staff'), Schwertleite ('sword-bearing'), a term used in the Middle Ages for 'entry into knighthood'; Rossweisse ('white steed') is a confusion with the name Hrotsvitha, which signifies something quite different ('fame — strong').
[15] 'Sintolt der Hegeling' gets his name from a court official in the *Nibelungenlied* and his patronymic from a leading tribe in *Kudrun*. 'Wittig der Irmin' is a concoction from the late medieval German epics where a Witege is the minion of a King Ermenrich.
[16] A slightly inaccurate interpretation by Wagner: the name components originally signified 'victory' and 'protection', i.e. 'preserve victory!'
[17] The components of Brünnhilde's name signify 'armour' and 'conflict'; in Old Norse, however, hildr acquires the secondary meaning of 'valkyrie'; thus her name could signify 'valkyrie in armour', which could have inspired the creation of the warrior-maiden sleeping on the mountain top. In the *Nibelungenlied* Brünnhild is an unromantic amazonian figure who fades from the scene after Siegfried's murder.
[18] Wagner would have known from Wilhelm Grimm's *Heldensage* that a rock on the Feldberg in the Taunus had been called 'Brunehildestein' in the past.
[19] The name Loge is Wagner's Germanisation of the name of Loki, the intelligent trickster god of Scandinavian mythology. Following Grimm, he has relatd the name to German Lohe, 'glow, flame'.

Translating 'The Ring'

Andrew Porter

This translation of *The Ring* was made for singing, acting, and hearing, not for reading. It is neither a straight, literal crib to the sense of the German such as, in our day, Peggie Cochrane, William Mann, and Lionel Salter[1] (see Notes and References at the end of this essay) have ably provided nor an attempt to render Wagner's verse into English verse such as an English translator-poet uncumbered by the need to frame his lines to fit Wagner's music might make. With unfeigned diffidence I offer to the eyes of a reader, rather than to the ears of a listener, a version that has been shaped by the rhythms, inflexions, weights, lengths, and sounds of Wagner's score. To someone who remarks 'This phrase doesn't translate the German at all precisely' or asks 'Why this rude inversion?' I can reply 'No literal translation would fit the musical phrase' and 'The harmony required those words in that order'. But to prove it a score is needed. This translation is incomplete until it meets the music. But people have asked to see it. It is over a century since the first rhythmic translation of a *Ring* opera — Alfred Forman's *The Walkyrie*, which appeared in 1873 — was printed.[2] It found many successors. And there is perhaps something to be said for as well as against English versions that attempt to convey the sense of Wagner's lines while moving in the measure of his verse.

The translator who chooses his own metre has an easier task. In blank verse (varied by 'lyrics' for the Rhinemaidens, the forging Siegfried, the Woodbird, the awakened Brünnhilde, and the Norns), Oliver Huckel[3] endeavoured 'to transfuse into English the very spirit of Wagner's lofty thought'. In his preface he declared that 'The usual English librettos of *The Ring* are totally

Alberto Remedios as Siegmund, Clifford Grant as Hunding and Margaret Curphey as Sieglinde at ENO in 1975 (photo: John Garner)

inadequate and confusing as translations of Wagner's text. They are made to suit the musical requirements rather than to present the thought in literary form. It is often a perplexing task rather than a pleasure to read them. Tenfold more involved and obscure than Browning, they have none of his redeeming grace of thought or speech.'

Dr Huckel was the author of *Through England with Tennyson*, of *Mental Medicine*, and of *Spiritual Surgery* (*Some Pointed Analogies between Body and Soul*). The concerns evinced in the latter titles gave him a clear grasp of the moral and psychological parables of *The Ring*, and Tennyson was his poetic model. Two brief excerpts will show the flavour. From Act One of *The Valkyrie*:

> But Siegmund shook himself, and springing up
> From the rude bearskin, spake with new-found strength:
> 'My wounds? Speak not of them — they are no more;
> Again I feel my strength in every limb.
> Yea, had my shield and spear been strong as now
> This strong right arm, ne'er had I fled my foes;
> But spear and shield were shattered, foes pressed sore . . .'

And, from the final scene of the cycle:

> Upon her steed, impetuous she leaped,
> And for the last time sounding forth the cry:
> 'Hoyotoho!' — her dear old Valkyr call —
> She bounded headlong in the flaming pyre.

Huckel's *Ring*, published in New York, appeared between 1907 and 1911. In England, Reginald Rankin, B.A., of the Inner Temple, Barrister-at-law, had already produced a version in blank verse (1899),[4] and Randall Fynes another (two volumes, 1899 and 1901),[5] interspersed, like Huckel's, with a few lyrics. Fynes declared it 'astonishing . . . that the attempt seems never to have been made before'; earlier versions are either fettered to the original metre or else mere paraphrases 'in most cases . . . told in the language of the nursery'. He himself uses the language of Tennyson, and adopts the conceit of an epic tale told on successive nights by a medieval bard. In passages like

> And then there came,
> Borne on the night, a faint and distant cry,
> As from beyond the limit of the World,
> Like a chill wind that blows in a waste land,
> Moaning, and crying, 'The Great Gods are dead!'

the specific allusions (in this case to *The Passing of Arthur*) are, in the manner of T.S. Eliot's *The Waste Land*, identified.

Early paraphrases 'in the language of the nursery' I have not examined. In 1903, E.F. Benson produced *The Valkyries*, a rendering in flummery prose.[6] Two prose versions of the thirties are hardly worth examination. C.L. LeMassena's[7] begins: '"Time for our morning dip," exclaims Woglinda'. Gertrude Henderson's[8] mingles baby-talk with fancy words: 'Clump, clump. The black heads of the Giants lifted above the shag of the mountain side. Clump, clump they came, until they stood in the presence of the Aesir.' John Updike's more recent version[9] is a bedtime tale for children clearly and quickly told. It takes ingenious advantage of Wagner's 'recapitulations', jumping from the end of *Das Rheingold* to the Mime-Wanderer riddle scene; the action of *Die Walküre* is related in those questions and answers and by the Wanderer's informing Siegfried, at the foot of the mountain, that he has 'fired' Brünnhilde — a nice word-play — for insubordination. *Götterdämmerung* gets only three sentences: Siegfried and Brünnhilde 'did not live happily ever after. No human beings do. In time they died, and in dying returned the Ring to the mermaids of the Rhine.' These versions are all abundantly illustrated. So — famously, by Arthur Rackham — is Margaret Armour's,[10] which is in verse that has a syllabic equivalence, more or less, to the original but does not lend itself to singing.

What of the singing versions? When Albert Forman sent his first (privately printed) translation of *The Walkyrie* to the Master, in 1873, he said: 'I trust that the day is not distant when an edition of the music with English words will become necessary . . . . I have compared the whole with the music, and I think a very few alterations of the words would fit them to appear with the score.' But when the first German/English vocal scores of *The Ring* appeared, from Schott, in the early 1880s, the translation was that of H. and F. Corder.[11] F. was the composer and conductor Frederick Corder, and H. his wife Henrietta Louisa, *née* Walford.

Forman's first aim had been to keep the alliteration. It led him to lines like:

on the steadfast pair of thy eyes, —	from dread wildering darkness, —
that so oft were stars of my storm,	for latest healing
when hope was fierce	here I must lean
in my heart like fire,	in last farewell
when world's-delightwards	of lingering lips!
my will was lifted	

(Dr Huckel's comments quoted above are plainly not unfair.) The Corders also strove to preserve the *Stabreim* — but less rigorously, and with happier results:

these effulgent, glorious eyes	from wild warfare were turning: —
whose flash my gloom oft dispell'd	their lustrous gaze
when hopeless cravings	lights on me now,
my heart discouraged,	as my lips imprint
or when my wishes	this last farewell!
toward worldly pleasure	

The Corders' *Valkyrie* was sung six times at Covent Garden in 1895, with a largely American cast. The following season the opera was done there in French!

Wagner himself is said to have disliked the Corders' translation. At the end of the century, Schott published new bilingual vocal scores, with English words by Frederick Jameson,[12] and the Jameson version has remained in the Schott and, in America, G. Schirmer editions ever since. It was heard in 1908 when Hans Richter gave Covent Garden its first complete English *Ring*, and as late as 1948, in a *Valkyrie* there with Kirsten Flagstad and Hans Hotter; and it has often been performed elsewhere. Jameson's version sings well and sounds well:

those gleaming, radiant eyes	through wild, wildering sadness:
that oft in storms on me shone,	once more to-day,
when hopeless yearning	lured by their light,
my heart had wasted,	my lips shall give them
when world's delights	love's farewell!
all my wishes wakened,	

When all Wagner's music entered the public domain, in 1914, Breitkopf & Härtel undertook a new, complete edition, and for the Breitkopf vocal scores

Ernest Newman made a new English translation,[13] along lines similar to Jameson's:

those unclouded glorious eyes,	by fear fettered and maddened —
that oft have lighted my gloom,	their gleam once more
when hopeless longing	gladdens me now,
my heart had wasted,	as my lips meet thine
when worldly pleasures	in love's last kiss.
I wished to win me,	

The first *Ring* in America, built up at the Metropolitan Opera between 1885 and 1888, was assembled in 1889. In New York, F. Rullman, the main provider of librettos, had already published some bilingual texts, with line-for-line but non-metrical translations by John P. Jackson, back in 1877 (when *Die Walküre* had its American première, at the New York Academy of Music). Rullman replaced at least *Siegfried* with the Corder version in the 1880s,[14] and brought out Charles Henry Meltzer's translations of *Das Rheingold* and *Die Walküre* in 1904. Another, uncredited — and discreditable — translation appeared in the vocal scores edited by Henry T. Finck and published by the John Church Co., of Cincinnati, in 1903. But the earlier American *Ring* translations, often reprinted,[15] and usually unattributed, form a tangled and unprofitable study. The information about them above is scrappy — but there are better ways of spending time than ploughing through and comparing the numerous 'theatre libretti' scattered in many libraries throughout America. The first significant and independent singing version produced in America is Stewart Robb's, of 1960.[16]

Robb set out 'to translate *The Ring* into clear, understandable modern English, avoiding obscurities of expression and archaic words ... yet preserving the rhythms of the original German where possible, and even some of the alliterative effects ... Here', he concludes, 'is a new English version of

Alberto Remedios (Siegmund) and Margaret Curphey (Sieglinde) at ENO in 1975 (photo: John Garner)

Der Ring des Nibelungen which can be enjoyed by the general reader as well as sung on the opera stage . . . Withal, it does not sound like a translation, but as though already written in English.' (Or written in American, an English reader may remark, as he comes across 'slowpoke', ''fraid-cat', a Mime who has 'fixed' soup for Siegfried, and — for Waltraute's *'Bist du von Sinnen?'* — 'Have you gone crazy?') I admire Robb's work but find it mixty-maxty: his vocabulary ranges from the colloquialisms quoted, through 'Frolic, good fellows' and 'He blows a rollicking horn', to 'Wish-maid', 'lot-chooser', and 'hest'. Wagner's tone varies widely, but Robb's more widely still. Fricka's measured *'Die Walküre wend auch von ihm!'* becomes 'Just keep Brunnhild out of his way'; but in the previous act of *The Valkyrie*, when Sieglinde pushes the hair back from Siegmund's forehead, her diction is surprisingly formal:

How wide and open	holds me entranced.
gleams your brow.	A wonder takes my attention:
Your temple displays	Before this time we met
all the interlaced veins.	my eyes had seen your face!
I tremble and my captive	

Some of the differences between Robb's modern version and mine can be more readily shown by quotation than defined. My Fricka says 'The Valkyrie leaves him to die!', and my Sieglinde:

Your noble brow	of my delight!
is broad and clear;	A marvel stirs in my memory:
its delicate veins	although you came but today,
with my fingers I trace!	I've seen your face before!
I tremble with the rapture	

And in doing so she lifts two lines ('I tremble with the rapture/of my delight!') directly from Jameson. Robb's Sieglinde is closer to the Corders', who sang 'I tremble with emotion / resting entranced!' (The German is *'Mir zagt es vor der Wonne / die mich entzückt!'*) In fact, one soon discovers that all *Ring* translators — after the pioneering Forman — have leant on the work of their predecessors. This is reasonable and right; in any case, the ways of translating a short sentence in tempo are not limitless. Compare: 'Who art thou, stalwart stripling, that hath struck my heart?' (Corders); 'Who art thou, valiant stripling, that hast pierced my breast?' (Jameson); again, 'Who art thou, valiant stripling, that has pierced my breast?' (Newman); 'Who are you, valiant stripling, that have pierced my heart?' (Robb); and 'Who are you, youthful hero, who have pierced my breast?' (Porter, who didn't care for 'stripling', especially since its first syllable must be sustained). My indebtedness to the Corders, Jameson, Newman, and Robb is great, and gratefully owned. I worked in full knowledge of their translations. When I was stuck, I turned to see what they had done. They suggested useful words, turns of phrase, syntactical short-cuts out of the thicket, and sometimes — not often, though I have chosen to quote an example above — whole lines that I could steal for my own purposes. I hope the next translator of *The Ring* finds my version similarly useful.

* * *

When the Sadler's Wells (now English National) Opera invited me to prepare a new English text for *The Ring*, I looked at these earlier singing versions to see whether there was really room for a new translation — and decided that perhaps there was. I thought it might be possible to try for something a little more fluent and direct, a little easier to understand, than Jameson or Newman had been, and also — this is where my version differs from most of its predecessors — a translation more closely bound to the details of the music, more accurately reflecting and not contradicting the melodic and harmonic 'articulations' of its phrases. I did the Annunciation of Death scene, in Act Two of *The Valkyrie*, as a test piece; Sadler's Wells approved, and I went ahead. The large inducement was that the musical interpretation, the production, and the translation, would be created together, by a team of British artists new to *The Ring*, inspired by Reginald Goodall, whom I revered as the greatest of living Wagnerian interpreters. The rehearsals were long, and at every stage the conductor, the producers, the musical coaches, and the singers themselves made suggestions that helped to provide a more comprehensible, singable, dramatic and 'musical' text.

Opera translations intended for singing have a limited life. Whether the translator of, say, an eighteenth-century opera chooses to employ a neutral and 'timeless' or a mock-eighteenth-century idiom, his work is likely to bear the stamp of the time it was made. It is easy to date to a decade or so a photograph of a soprano dressed, wigged, and painted as Mozart's Countess Almaviva or Richard Strauss's Feldmarschallin. Similarly, in the 1980s one can distinguish between 'eighteenth-century English' written in the 1850s, the 1890s, and the 1930s. After perhaps a century, a translation made at the time of an opera's composition, possibly under its composer's eye, may well acquire a certain 'period authenticity' and warrant revival — though this is not the case with, for example, the standard Italian translations of Verdi's *Les Vêpres siciliennes* and *Don Carlos*. In the former, fiery sentiments such as Giovanni da Procida's cry of *'la liberté!'* were quenched, to avoid clashes with Italian censorship, and in both, Verdi, too permissive with his translators, allowed fine dramatic and fine musical points to be blunted. In any event, French-into-Italian is hard. Masculine endings are feminized; *fort* becomes *forte* and *Elisabeth, Elisabetta*. Once upon a time, poetic usage permitted the dropping of final syllables; *destin cruel* could move south as *destin crudel* rather than *destino crudele*. But now, as Gian Carlo Menotti has remarked, a modern Italian librettist is more or less committed to feminine phrase endings except when his characters visit the *città* to drink a *caffè*.

Italian-into-French is somewhat easier. French-into-English raises constant problems of how to treat not-quite-mute - *e*. Italian-into-English often results in phrase after phrase ending with an accusative pronoun: *Soccorso!* becomes *Oh help me!*, and *Son tradita!, He betrayed me!* Moreover, all English translators, from whatever language, tend to keep on hand a box filled with *thens* and *nows* into which they can dip to fill out their lines. Since Italians take four syllables to bid one another goodnight, Sparafucile, Preziosilla and the rest usually say *Well, goodnight then!*

German characters on the English lyric stage usually say *So, goodnight*. The difficulties of German-into-English are rather different, and in the case of *Ring*-into-English they are compounded by Wagner's *Stabreim* or alliteration, his hard syntax, and his archaic vocabulary. For many of the recurrent key words there are syllabic equivalents. *Blut* is *blood*, *Schwert* is *sword*, and *Tod* is *death*. *Liebe* and *Auge* give more trouble; on a few occasions the singers of my *Ring*-in-English are asked to slur two notes to *love* and *eye*, and Fafner the *Wurm* was not easily transformed into a *dragon*. But syllabic equivalents are not sonic equivalents: the long, dark vowels of a sustained *Blut* or *Tod* are illrepresented by *blood* and *death*. A German Siegmund can cry *Schwert* with a bright, forward ring that a mere *sword* is powerless to provide. Although *vengeance* is a word that can be said vehemently, *Rache* is more powerfully a

Rita Hunter as Brünnhilde, Norman Bailey as Wotan, and the Valkyries at ENO in 1970 (photo: Anthony Crickmay)

swift double explosion. If all British and American singers, conductors, producers, and designers of *The Ring* and all their audiences commanded, not just German, but specifically Wagner's strange German as a second language — if, using the original words, the singers could express themselves fully and be sure of being understood, in detail, by those who heard them — there would be no call to translate *The Ring* into English. As one of its translators, I am dismayed when I compare, say Wagner's:

Wie liebliche Luft	Traurig ging es uns allen,
wieder uns weht,	getrennt für immer von ihr,
wonnig Gefühl	die leidlos ewiger Jugend
die Sinne erfüllt!	jubelnde Lust uns verleiht

— Froh's 'arietta' in the last scene of *Das Reingold* — with my:

How sweetly the air	Life indeed would be wretched
charms us again;	if we were parted from her;
joy and contentment	she brings us youth eternal,
steal through my heart!	fills us with joy and delight.

But there were compensations. When I heard Rita Hunter fill even so stilted a phrase as 'You who this love in my heart inspired' with tender, swelling emotion, Ava June utter Sieglinde's long solo that begins 'My husband's kinsmen', Norman Bailey 'think aloud' in Wotan's monologue, and Alberto Remedios relate Siegfried's young adventures, to audiences that followed what was said, I could believe there had been some gains as well as the inevitable and enormous losses.

All translation is a matter of weighing gains and losses. *The Ring* — despite what some German critics of Wagner's verse may feel — is not one of the works of which it can be said, as it was of James Fennimore Cooper's novels, that they have been 'often translated, never without improvement'. In the lyric theatre, the gains are in verbal and dramatic communicativeness. (Has there ever been a great composer who did not prefer his works to be performed in the language of the country?) The losses are of that other 'sense' conveyed by the sound and the untranslatable subtleties of the original words. And the translator's task is to make such losses as light as possible. I began work on *The Ring* without theories, almost instinctively — holding the sound of a German phrase in my ears and the literal sense of it in my mind, and rejecting version after version until I hit on English words that seemed to fit. Much later — when *The Valkyrie* was almost finished — I realized that I had been guided by six different, linked, and for the most part mutually unachievable intentions.

(1) To provide a translation that is close to the original and at the same time makes audible sense at first hearing, without needing to be 'worked out' by a puzzled listener. Towards the close of *The Rhinegold*, Fricka, hearing the name Walhall for the first time, asks what it means. The Corders' Wotan replied: 'What might 'gainst our fears my mind may have found, if proved a success, soon shall explain that name.' And Forman's: 'What, in might over fear, my manfulness found, shall matchlessly live and lead the meaning to light'. Both are fair representations of some tortuous German. But I felt that unless the meaning could be led to light a little more directly than that, the speech might as well be left in German. So, natural words in a natural order.

(2) To keep important words — such as *Liebe, Leid, Ring, Rhein* — and especially the proper names exactly where Wagner placed them. Their sounds and rhythms often have a motivic significance; they coincide with particular harmonies. In my first draft, instead of that stilted phrase of Brünnhilde's quoted above, I had the more direct 'You who inspired me to feel this love'. Reginald Goodall pointed out that the chord on the fourth syllable was inseparable from *Liebe*; hence, 'You who this love in my heart inspired,' which reads less well but makes far better musical sense. For the same reason, Brünnhilde's 'One thing I did know, that you still loved the Wälsung', a little earlier, was changed to '. . . that the Wälsung you loved'.

(3) To keep, wherever possible, the *Stabreim*, as an essential part of the patterning in the score's structure.

(4) To echo the sound of the German — the ring of bright, forward vowels, the full shadows cast by dark ones, the attack of hammer-stroke consonants, the hiss and splutter of certain sibilant sequences. (Wagner's invented language is richer in long vowels and percussive consonants than even modern German; it would be easier to translate its sounds into Old English or into Northumbrian dialect.) Sound sometimes took precedence of literal sense. For Alberich's 'Zertrümmert! Zerknickt!' (literally 'Destroyed! Crushed!'), Jameson has 'Defeated! Destroyed!' I made him 'Defeated! and tricked!'

(5) To reflect the differing tones, ranging from the elevated and rhetorical (notably Wotan's harangues in Act Three of *Die Walküre*), through Froh's — and Fasolt's — lyricism in *Das Rheingold*, to Loge's airy wit and Siegfried's boisterous sallies; to let such jokes as Siegfried and the Wanderer make be heard as such. The gods, Desmond Shawe-Taylor told me early on, shouldn't talk like the people next door. I hope mine do not — but I know he thinks that they have shed some of their dignity together with the second person singular. That form offered to the old translators a syllabic flexibility — *thou dost* or *doest, didest* or *didst* — denied to a modern translator who has decided, rightly or wrongly, against its use. He, on the other hand, is likely to gain new alternatives by resorting to contractions (*I have, I've*) more freely than they did. Wagner made liberal use of such contractions and elisions ('dir werf' ich's zu'; 'Ist's der, den du Gunther'n gab'st'), often introducing them when he came to set his written words to music. In English, I confess, similar forms sometimes strike too modern and colloquial a note, but I've used them when disruption of the musical rhythm (dividing, say, a minim on *I've* into two crotchets for *I have*) would be more disturbing still. They can look worse than they sound. When 'Do you think . . .?' is said quickly it becomes two syllables, 'D'you think', pronounced *Dew think*. Although the ear notices nothing

René Kollo as Siegmund at Covent Garden in 1976 (photo: Donald Southern)

amiss, an eye seeing it thus written would be distressed. And so for that eye's sake I have once or twice in this printed text spelt out in full what in performance is meant to be elided. However, the frequent omission of the final -*e* of Brünnhilde, Gutrune, etc., is not a misprint but Wagner's practice; and Nibelung and Niblung are his alternatives.

(6) Most important of all — sometimes I felt that, like Brünnhilde, *im Auge das eine ich hielt* and ignored all other imperatives — to find words that fit the music closely. Take the last two lines of that passage from Wotan's farewell quoted above in Forman's, the Corders' Jameson's, and Newman's versions. The German is 'mit dem Lebewohles/letztem Kuss'; -*woh*- is a B suspended over an F major chord, and -*les* is its resolution on to A; then there is a semiquaver rest, a small break, before *letztem Kuss*. Only Jameson's lines fit the music. Forman's give us, in effect, 'farewellov/lingering lips'; the Corders' 'imprint-this/last farewell'; and Newman's 'thine-in/love's last kiss'. Robb has 'brief and final/farewell kiss', which fits well enough — but is Wotan's kiss really 'brief'? (My version — to save any curious reader from paging on — is 'loving,/last farewell'.) Or take the opening words of Brünnhilde's immolation scene, '*Starke Scheite/schichtet mir dort*'. One old translation, 'Mighty faggots', will plainly not do today. But for other reasons Jameson's 'mighty logs I' (*log's eye*) and Robb's 'Let great logs be' (*Great Logsby*, inflected like the *Great Gatsby*) must be deemed unfitting. Even though the soprano may draw no breath between the lines, the declamation is wrong. Insufficient care about such points of declamation, I believe, has done much to give opera-in-English its reputation of 'sounding awful'. Earlier *Ring* translations contain things like Sieglinde's 'And his packper/Sue in mighty force', Siegmund's 'What has ensnared/Me now well I know', Wotan's 'A lu—ckier manwill/Joy in thy stars' (*lu*- sustained, *man will* given the inflexion of *mandrill*), and Brünnhilde's:

> The world's most glorious hear,
> Roe-bears, o woo,
> Man thy shell, tering womb!

There are some things like that in my version but, I hope, not many. I can think of no English phrase that correctly 'articulates' the awakening Brünnhilde's '*Heil dir, Sonne!*' except 'Hi there, sunshine!' — and that won't do. (So each Brünnhilde, with her conductor, has chosen, from a list of variously unsatisfactory compromises provided, the version she finds least unmusical.) Most of the revisions undertaken after hearing the translation in performances have been directed towards obtaining a better musical fit.

A seventh requirement is conspicuously absent from those above: any attempt to reflect what Martin Cooper has called 'the cloudy, archaic literary style that was an organic part of Wagner's mystique.'[17] Deliberately so. For I felt that anyone who wanted to listen to *The Ring* not-quite-understanding what is said could well listen to it, unspoiled, in the original cloudy German; what would be the point of devising yet another translation 'tenfold more involved and obscure than Browning'? So this is not a text acceptable to those who believe, with Mr Cooper, that the listener's attention should be 'lulled rather than altered by the words', that 'only the suspension of the intellectual processes will make him accept the time-scale which Wagner imposes'. It is a belief that I understand but do not fully share. From my first encounter with *The Ring*, I wanted to know exactly what all those characters were saying.

In any case, a translator cannot do everything. A glance at the following pages will reveal how very, very seldom even my 'six points' could all be met. Phrase by phrase, it was a matter of deciding which of them, in that particular

Katherine Pring as Fricka with Raimund Herincx as Wotan at ENO (photo: John Garner)

place, should be deemed paramount, of discovering which were achieveable at all, and then of settling for the least unsatisfactory, most singable in English. Often but not always the *Stabreim* was the first thing to go; intelligible and otherwise accurate words were usually preferred to fancier alternatives that happened to begin with the right letters. So, not 'Notung! Notung! needfullest sword!' or 'Needful! Needful! notable sword!' (Corders). And, for other reasons, not 'Notung! Notung! conquering sword!' (Jameson) or 'Needful! Needful! conquering sword!' (Robb's amalgam of Corders and Jameson). I chose this example (I have 'Notung! Notung! sword of my need!') because it brings up another recurrent 'crux' — the proper names, which in *The Ring* always mean something. The Valkyries' function — choosing those slain in battle — is defined by their name. In *The Ring*, I would be a doorkeeper. Valkyrie has been an English word since the eighteenth century, and so I used it. But so has Valhalla, the hall of those slain in battle; musical reasons, however, predicate the two syllables of Wagner's *Walhall*. I could have spelt it with a *V* — but that could lead to Votan, Vellgunde, and Valtrauta. (Lord Acton, who told Mr Gladstone that 'neither Pitt nor Peel lives in my Walhalla', provides some precedent for keeping the *W* even in English.) On the whole I have left the names and the puns that are made upon them untranslated. Siegmund and Sieglinde could hardly be Victor and gentle Vicky. My *'Wehwalt der Wölfing'* is not 'Woeful the Wolf-cub'. And if, at the Coliseum, Hunding (as in Robb) were to call out 'Woe-King! Woe-King!' in Act Two of *The Valkyrie*, a British audience's reaction might be: 'Next stop, Basingstoke'. But sometimes I tried to gloss: 'I'm Wehwalt, named for my sorrow'; 'Siegfried, victorious and free' for *'Siegfried erfreu sich des Siegs!'*, when Brünnhilde tells Sieglinde the name of her son-to-be. (*Free* may not be in the German, but it does point towards *den Freien* whom Wotan has longed for, and it also keeps Wagner's vowel.) About orthography I have been inconsistent. 'Hoyotoho!' gives a reasonable approximation to the sounds wanted, but things like Rhinemaidens' 'Wallala weiala' defeated me — *viala* is sonically ambiguous, and any attempts to show that the *i* is long began to suggest Viyella — so I left them in German spelling. As in most prints of the German libretto since Breitkopf's, I have omitted the unsounded *h* in *Not(h)*, *Not(h)ung* etc., and many of the apostrophes indicating Wagner's elided *e's*. *Rhinegold* (like rhinestone) is so well established in English usage as one word that to transform it into *Rhine Gold*, as some advised, seemed to me pedantic.

*   *   *

The Ring is on the first level a rousing and splendid old tale of gods and dwarfs and men, of giants and dragons, loves and hates, murder, magic, and mysteries, unfolded amid vast and picturesque scenery. Beyond that, it is about (among other things) man's conquest of the natural world for his own uses (the first action recorded is Wotan's tearing a branch from the World Ashtree); about man's dominion over men (well-intentioned oligarchy and capitalist tyranny are both condemned); and about man's understanding of himself (the forces influencing his action, at the start located in gods, are finally discovered to lie within himself). By intention, Wagner patterned his drama on Attic tragedy but chose as his symbolic matter the ancestral myths of the North. To mankind's collective unconsciousness he gave form; that is easily said, but for that matter it can easily — if not briefly — be demonstrated. Instinct, inspiration, the composer's comprehensive grasp of what men before him had thought, dreamed, and done, and his powerful controlling mind directed the creation of *The Ring* over more than a quarter-century. In words, music, and vivid theatrical imagery combined it took shape.

Each of the clauses above has been the subject of many books; I mention here these large matters in summary form only to make the point, that believing *all* these things about *The Ring* to be true, I have not endeavoured to translate it with special reference to any one of them. This is not a particular 'interpretation'. Such interpretations — usually they are the work of ambitious producers, who have determined to disassemble the components of the *Gesamtkunstwerk* — can cast exciting new light on aspects of the work. They can be maddening. And, however brilliant, they are achieved only by diminishing the force and richness of the whole.

For five years, scores of *The Ring* accompanied me wherever I went — *wo ich mich fand, wohin ich zog*. Some lines now always recall places: the Kent garden where a tricky line of Sieglinde's was suddenly solved; a journey from Coimbra to Lisbon during which the Fricka-Wotan argument of *The Valkyrie* fell into place; the Glasgow hotel bedroom where all day long I worked at translating, leaving at night to hear — in German — Scottish Opera's *Ring*; and, above all, William Weaver's farmhouse in the Tuscan hills, where much of the work was done. My debts are great, and of many kinds: as I have said, to several previous translators; to Kirsten Flagstad, Astrid Varnay, Hans Hotter, Ludwig Weber, Wilhelm Furtwängler, Hans Knappertsbusch, Rudolf Kempe, and all those who taught me how *The Ring* could sound; to Reginald Goodall, Glen Byam Shaw and John Blatchley, John Barker, Edmund Tracey, Leonard Hancock, and all the singers who worked on the Sadler's Wells production, *in langer Zeiten Lauf*, refining my phrases and bringing them to life; to George London, who, while producing this English *Ring* in several American cities, made helpful new suggestions; to critical colleagues — especially David Cairns, Bernard Levin, Max Loppert, Peter Stadlen, and David Hamilton — who encouraged me; and to Claire Brook, without whose help I could never have got the thing into print at all.

Notes

1. Peggie Cochrane's translation appeared with the Decca recordings conducted by Georg Solti. William Mann's was published (in short lines) by the Friends of Covent Garden, in 1964, and later (with Wagner's lineation) to accompany the EMI recording conducted by Furtwängler. Lionel Salter's translations of *Das Rheingold*, *Siegfried*, and *Götterdämmerung* accompanied the Deutsche Grammophon recordings conducted by Karajan (for *Die Walküre*, the Mann version was used).

2. Alfred Forman: *The Walkyrie* (privately printed, London, 1873); *The Nibelung's Ring, English words to Richard Wagner's Ring des Nibelungen, in the alliterative verse of the original* (London: Schott, 1877).

3. Oliver Huckel: *The Rhine-Gold, A Dramatic Poem by Richard Wagner freely translated into poetic narrative form* (New York: Thomas Y. Crowell, 1907); followed by *The Valkyrie* (1909), *Siegfried* (1910), and *The Dusk of the Gods* (1911) — and by all Wagner's other dramas, from *Rienzi* to *Parsifal*.

4. Reginald Rankin: *Wagner's Nibelungen Ring done into English verse* (London: Longmans, Green, 1899, 2 vols).

5. Randle Fynes: *The Ring of the Nibelung, An English version* (London: Smith, Elder, 1899-1901, 2 vols; 1913, one-volume edition).

6. E.F. Benson: *The Valkyries, A Romance* (London: T. Fisher Unwin, 1903).

7. C.E. LeMassena: *The Ring of the Nibelung* (New York: Grossman-Roth, 1930).

8. Gertrude Henderson: *The Ring of the Nibelung* (New York: Alfred A. Knopf, 1932).

9. John Updike: *The Ring* (New York: Alfred A. Knopf, 1964).

10. Margaret Armour: *The Ring of the Niblung . . . translated into English* (London: Wm. Heinemann, 1911, 2 vols).

11. The only firmly dated Corder vocal score I have seen is a *Götterdämmerung* of 1881. The plate number of the German/English *Rheingold* is 23504, of *Die Walküre* 23188; 1882 is the date usually assigned to the vocal scores and the bilingual libretti.

12. Frederick Jameson: *The Nibelung's Ring, English words to Richard Wagner's Ring des Nibelungen, An accurate translation* (London: Schott, 1896). This was followed at the turn of the century by individual bilingual libretti and by vocal scores from both Schott and G. Schirmer. The Jameson version also appears in the Schott and Eulenburg miniature scores.

13. Newman's translations of *The Rhinehold* and *The Valkyrie* had already been published in London, in 1912, as Nos. 4 and 5 of Breitkopf & Härtel's Textbooks. The vocal scores are in the Hofmeister catalogue for the years 1914-18.

14. The Corder translations were also reprinted by C.F. Tretbar, of New York, in 1893, and by Oliver Ditson, of Boston, in 1904.

15. For example, as late as 1938 *The Authentic Librettos of the Wagner Operas* (New York: Crown Publishers) gathers in facsimile four different 'theatre libretti' (*Siegfried* with cuts and all) in different type-faces — basically the Corders' text, mingled with some Meltzer prefatory material.

16. Stewart Robb: *The Ring of the Nibelung* (New York: Dutton, 1960); English only; useful introductory essays by Edward Downes and by the translator. Published as individual, bilingual libretti by G. Schirmer. (I have not seen Walter Ducloux's unpublished singing translation of *Das Rheingold*.)

17. Martin Cooper: 'Wagner without the wizardry', *Daily Telegraph*, August 18, 1973.

Thematic Guide

Each Opera Guide to a part of *The Ring* refers to one general list of leitmotifs in which the themes are numbered according to their first appearance in the cycle. Only the principal ones that occur in *The Valkyrie* are given here.

51

Siegmund's fight with Hunding as depicted by the Illustrirte Zeitung, Leipsig, 1876.

The Valkyrie
Die Walküre

First Day of the Festival Play
'The Ring of the Nibelung'

Music-Drama by Richard Wagner
Poem by Richard Wagner
English Translation by Andrew Porter
with a footnote to Act Two translated by Elizabeth Forbes

The Valkyrie was first performed in Munich on June 26, 1870. It was first performed at the Festspielhaus, Bayreuth, on August 14, 1876. The first performance in America was in New York on April 2, 1877. The first performance in London was at Covent Garden on October 16, 1895.

This translation was commissioned by English National Opera (then Sadler's Wells Opera) and first performed at the London Coliseum on January 29, 1970. The full cycle was first given in July and August, 1973 and the opera was recorded in performance at the London Coliseum in December 1975 by EMI.

The German text for the whole cycle was first published in 1853. Archaisms of spelling and an excess of punctuation have been removed but the original verse layout has been retained.

The stage directions are literal translations of those written by Wagner and do not reflect any actual production. The numbers in square brackets refer to the Thematic Guide.

Siegmund		*tenor*
Hunding		*bass*
Wotan		*bass-baritone*
Sieglinde		*soprano*
Brünnhilde		*soprano*
Fricka		*soprano*
Gerhilde		*soprano*
Ortlinde		*soprano*
Waltraute		*contralto*
Schwertleite		*contralto*
Helmwige	*Valkyries*	*soprano*
Siegrune		*contralto*
Grimgerde		*contralto*
Rossweise		*contralto*

Maria Muller as Sieglinde (Royal Opera House Archives)

Act One

Inside a dwelling. In the middle stands a mighty ash-tree, whose prominent roots spread wide and lose themselves in the ground. The summit of the tree is cut off by a jointed roof, so pierced that the trunk and the boughs branching out on every side pass through it, through openings made exactly to fit. We assume that the top of the tree spreads out above the roof. Around the trunk of the ash, as central point, a room has been constructed. The walls are of rudely hewn wood, here and there hung with plaited and woven rugs. In the foreground, right, is a hearth, whose chimney goes up sideways to the roof; behind the hearth is an inner room, like a storeroom, reached by a few wooden steps. In front of it, half-drawn, is a plaited hanging. In the background, an entrance-door with a simple wooden latch. Left, the door to an inner chamber, similarly reached by steps. Further forward, on the same side, a table with a broad bench fastened to the wall behind it and wooden stools in front of it.

Scene One. *A short orchestral prelude of violent, stormy character introduces the scene.* [26] *When the curtain rises, Siegmund, from without, hastily opens the main door and enters.* [28] *It is towards evening; a fierce thunderstorm is just about to die down. For a moment, Siegmund keeps his hand on the latch and looks around the room; he seems to be exhausted by tremendous exertions; his raiment and general appearance proclaim him a fugitive. Seeing no one, he closes the door behind him, walks to the hearth, and throws himself down there, exhausted, on a bearskin rug.* [5]

SIEGMUND

The storm drove me here; here I must shelter.	[28]	Was Herd dies auch sei, hier muss ich rasten.

(He sinks back and remains for a while stretched out, motionless. Sieglinde enters from the door of the inner room, thinking that her husband has returned. Her grave look changes to one of surprise when she sees a stranger on the hearth.)

SIEGLINDE
(still at the back)

A stranger here? Where has he come from?	[5]	Ein fremder Mann? Ihn muss ich fragen.

(Quietly, she comes a few steps closer.)

Who sought this house, and lies by the fire?	[28]	Wer kam ins Haus und liegt dort am Herd?

(As Siegmund does not move, she comes a little closer and looks at him.)

He's exhausted and makes no move. Can he have fainted there, or is he dead?	Müde liegt er von Weges Mühn: schwanden die Sinne ihm? Wäre er siech?

(She bends over him and listens.) [29, 28]

Ah no, he is breathing; it seems that he's sleeping. Valiant, strong is the man, though he's weary now.	Noch schwillt ihm der Atem; das Auge nur schloss er. Mutig dünkt mich der Mann, sank er müd auch hin.

SIEGMUND
(suddenly raises his head) [28]

A drink! A drink!	Ein Quell! Ein Quell!

SIEGLINDE

I'll bring some water.	Erquickung schaff ich.

(She quickly takes a drinking-horn and goes out of the house with it. Returning with it filled, she offers it to Siegmund.) [28, 29]

Cool your lips with this drink that I've brought you! Water — will you not drink?	Labung biet ich dem lechzenden Gaumen: Wasser, wie du gewollt!

SIEGMUND

(drinks and hands her back the horn. As he signals his thanks with his head, his glance fastens on her features with growing interest.) [30]

Cool and refreshing —		Kühlende labung
now I am well;	[29]	gab mir der Quell,
my load of care		des Müden Last
suddenly light;		machte er leicht;
my spirits revive;		erfrischt ist der Mut,
my eyes enjoy		das Aug' erfreut
a blessed, glorious sight.		des Sehens selige Lust.
And who has brought me to life?		[29] Wer ist's, der so mir es labt?

SIEGLINDE

This house and this wife		Dies Haus und dies Weib
belong to Hunding.		sind Hundings Eigen;
He will welcome his guest:		gastlich gönn' er dir Rast:
wait here till he returns.		[28] harre, bis heim er kehrt!

SIEGMUND

Weaponless am I:	Waffenlos bin ich:
a wounded guest	dem wunden Gast
cannot trouble your husband.	wird dein Gatte nicht wehren.

SIEGLINDE
(with anxious haste)

Oh quickly show me the wounds!   Die Wunden weise mir schnell!

SIEGMUND
(shakes himself and sits up quickly.)

A scratch merely,	Gering sind sie,
unworthy your care;	der Rede nicht wert;
no bone in my body	noch fügen des Leibes
broken at all.	Glieder sich fest.
Had my shield and spear been as strong,	Hätten halb so stark wie mein Arm
half as strong as my body,	Schild und Speer mir gehalten,
I would never have fled;	nimmer floh ich dem Feind;
but they shattered my spear and shield.	doch zerschellten mir Speer und Schild.
And so I fled	Der Feinde Meute
the enemy's rage;	hetzte mich müd,
a thunderstorm	Gewitterbrunst
broke overhead.	brach meinen Leib;
Yet, swifter than I was fleeing,	doch schneller, als ich der Meute,
all my faintness has fled.	[28] schwand die Müdigkeit mir;
Darkness had covered my eyes —	sank auf die Lider mir Nacht,
the sunlight smiles on me now.	[29] die Sonne lacht mir nun neu.

SIEGLINDE
(goes to the storeroom, fills a horn with mead, and offers it to Siegmund with friendly eagerness.)

I bring you a drink	[29]	Des seimigen Metes
of honeyed mead;		süssen Trank
say that you'll not refuse.		mögst du mir nicht verschmähn.

SIEGMUND

Will you not taste it first?   [30] Schmecktest du mir ihn zu?
(Sieglinde sips from the horn and gives it back to him. Siegmund takes a long draught, while his gaze rests on her with growing warmth. Still gazing, he takes the horn from his lips and lets it sink slowly, while the expression on his face tells of strong emotion. He sighs deeply, and gloomily lowers his gaze to the ground. With trembling voice:) [28]

Evil fortune's never far from me:	Einen Unseligen labtest du:
may I keep it	Unheil wende
away from you!	der Wunsch von dir!

(He starts up to go.)

I rested sweetly;	Gerastet hab ich
I feel refreshed.	und süss geruht:
I must go on my way.	weiter wend ich den Schritt.

(He moves towards the back.)

(turning round quickly)

Who pursues you? Why must you flee?   Wer verfolgt dich, dass du schon fliehst?

SIEGMUND
(arrested by her cry; slowly and sadly)

Ill fate pursues me,	Misswende folgt mir,
follows my footsteps;	wohin ich fliehe;
ill fate advances —	Misswende naht mir,
soon it will reach me.	wo ich mich zeige.
This ill fate you must not share!	[30b] Dir, Frau, doch bleibe sie fern!
So I must leave your house.	Fort wende ich Fuss und Blick.

(He strides swiftly to the door and lifts the latch.)

SIEGLINDE
(calling to him with impetuous self-forgetfulness)

No, do not leave!	So bleibe hier!
You bring no ill fate to me,	Nicht bringst du Unheil dahin,
for ill fate has long been here!	[31] wo Unheil im Hause wohnt!

SIEGMUND
(deeply moved, remains where he is; he gazes intently at Sieglinde, who lowers her eyes in embarrassment and sadness. A long silence. Siegmund returns into the room.)

Wehwalt, that is my name.	Wehwalt heiss ich mich selbst:
Hunding—I will await him.	[31, 29] Hunding will ich erwarten.

(He leans against the hearth; his eyes fix themselves with calm and steady sympathy on Sieglinde. Slowly, she raises her eyes again to his. They gaze into one another's eyes, during a long silence, with an expression of the deepest emotion.) [30b]

Scene Two. *Suddenly Sieglinde starts, listens, and hears Hunding, who is leading his horse to the stable outside. She goes quickly to the door and opens it. Hunding, armed with shield and spear, enters, and pauses at the threshold on perceiving Siegmund. He turns to Sieglinde with a glance of stern inquiry.* [32]

SIEGLINDE
(in answer to Hunding's look)

There he lay,	Müd am Herd
feeble and faint;	fand ich den Mann:
need drove him in here.	[28] Not führt' ihn ins Haus.

HUNDING

You cared for him?   Du labtest ihn?

SIEGLINDE

I said you'd welcome him;	Den Gaumen letzt' ich ihm,
greeted him as guest.	gastlich sorgt' ich sein!

SIEGMUND
(watching Hunding calmly and firmly)

Rest and drink,	Dach und Trank
both she brought:	dank ich ihr:
Why should you then reproach her?	willst du dein Weib drum schelten?

HUNDING

Sacred is my hearth;	Heilig ist mein Herd:
sacred keep you my house.	heilig sei dir mein Haus!

(He hands his weapons to Sieglinde, and says to her:) [32]

Go, make ready our meal!   Rüst uns Männern das Mahl!

(Sieglinde hangs the weapons on the branches of the ash-tree, fetches food and drink from the storeroom, and prepares the table for supper. Involuntarily she turns her eyes again to Siegmund. Hunding looks keenly and with astonishment at Siegmund's features, comparing them with his wife's; aside:) [29, 30a]

He looks like my wife there!	Wie gleicht er dem Weibe!
A glittering snake	Der gleissende Wurm
seems to shine in their glances.	glänzt auch ihm aus dem Auge.

57

(He hides his surprise and turns, as if unconcerned, to Siegmund.) [28, 32]

You have strayed	Weit her, traun,
far from your path;	kamst du des Wegs;
you rode no horse	ein Ross nicht ritt,
to reach my house.	der Rast hier fand:
What painful journey	welch schlimme Pfade
brought you to me?	schufen dir Pein?

SIEGMUND

Through field and forest,	Durch Wald und Wiese,
meadow and marsh,	Heide und Hain,
driven by storm	jagte mich Sturm
and starkest need —	und starke Not:
I know not the way that I took;	nicht kenn ich den Weg, den ich kam.
nor can I tell you	Wohin ich irrte,
where I have wandered.	weiss ich noch minder:
May I now learn it from you?	Kunde gewänn' ich des gern.

HUNDING
(at the table, motioning to Siegmund to sit)

This house is mine,	Des Dach dich deckt,
this land is mine;	des Haus dich hegt
Hunding is your host.	[32] Hunding heisst der Wirt;
Turn to the west	wendest von hier du
when you leave my house,	nach West den Schritt,
and there my kin	in Höfen reich
dwell in rich homesteads,	hausen dort Sippen
where Hunding's honour is guarded.	die Hundings Ehre behüten.
You may honour me too:	Gönnt mir Ehre mein Gast,
will my guest not tell me his name?	wird sein Name nun mir genannt.

(Siegmund, who has sat down at the table, gazes thoughtfully in front of him. Sieglinde has placed herself next to Hunding, opposite Siegmund, on whom she fastens her eyes with evident sympathy and intentness. Hunding, observing them both:) [30b, 31, 29]

Though you fear	Trägst du Sorge,
to trust it to me,	mir zu vertraun,
my wife here longs to hear it.	der Frau hier gib doch Kunde:
See, how eagerly she asks!	sieh, wie gierig sie dich frägt!

SIEGLINDE
(unembarrassed and eager)

Guest, I would know	Gast, wer du bist,
who you are.	wüst' ich gern.

SIEGMUND
(looks up, gazes into her eyes, and begins gravely.) [31]

Friedmund no one could call me;	Friedmund darf ich nicht heissen;
Frohwalt — would that I were!	Frohwalt möcht' ich wohl sein:
I'm Wehwalt, named for my sorrow.	doch Wehwalt muss ich mich nennen.
Wolfe, he was my father;	Wolfe, der war mein Vater;
his two children were twins —	zu zwei kam ich zur Welt,
my unhappy sister and I.	eine Zwillingsschwester und ich.
Both mother and sister	Früh schwanden mir
were lost —	Mutter und Maid;
my mother killed	die mich gebar
and my sister borne off —	und die mit mir sie barg,
taken while I was a boy.	kaum hab ich je sie gekannt.
Valiant and strong was Wolfe;	Wehrlich und stark war Wolfe;
his foes were many and fierce.	der Feinde wuchsen ihm viel.
And hunters bold	Zum Jagen zog
were the boy and his father.	mit dem Jungen der Alte:
Once, weary and worn,	von Hetze und Harst
we came from the chase,	einst kehrten sie heim:
and found our home laid waste.	da lag das Wolfsnest leer.
A heap of ash	Zu Schutt gebrannt
was all that was left;	der prangende Saal,
a stump where once	zum Stumpf der Eiche

58

an oak tree had stood;
the corpse of my mother
lay at my feet;
all trace of my sister
was lost in smoke.
This cruel blow was dealt
by ruffians who sought revenge.
As outlaws then
we took to the woods;
there I lived
with Wolfe my father;
in hunting I spent my youth.
Many a raid
was made on us both,
but we had learnt
to defend our lives.

blühender Stamm;
erschlagen der Mutter
mutiger Leib,
verschwunden in Gluten
der Schwester Spur.
Uns schuf die herbe Not
[32] der Neidinge harte Schar.
Geächtet floh
der Alte mit mir;
lange Jahre
lebte der Junge
mit Wolfe im wilden Wald:
Manche Jagd
ward auf sie gemacht;
doch mutig wehrte
das Wolfspaar sich.

(turning to Hunding)

A Wölfing tells you this tale,
and as 'Wölfing' often I'm known.

Ein Wölfing kündet dir das,
den als 'Wölfing' mancher wohl kennt.

[32]

HUNDING

Wonderful, wild adventures
came to our daring guest,
Wehwalt the Wölfing!
I think that I've heard of the pair,
I've heard unholy stories
spoken of Wolfe
and Wölfing too.

Wunder und wilde Märe
kündest du, kühner Gast,
Wehwalt, der Wölfing!
Mich dünkt, von dem wehrlichen Paar
vernahm ich dunkle Sage,
kannt' ich auch Wolfe
und Wölfing nicht.

SIEGLINDE

But tell us more, o stranger:
where is your father now?

Doch weiter künde, Fremder:
wo weilt dein Vater jetzt?

SIEGMUND

The ruffians raided again,
fell on my father and me;
and many hunters
fell in the battle;
they fled through the wood,
chased by us both;
like chaff we scattered the foe.
They parted my father from me;
in the fight I lost him.
A long while I sought him.
Though I found the wolf-skin
that he had worn,
no more could I find;
my father was not there.
Then I lost my love for the woods;
I mingled with warriors and women.
But all in vain,
often I tried
to find a friend,
to woo a maid —
everywhere I was rejected.
Ill fate lay on me.
For what I thought was right,
others reckoned was wrong,
and what seemed to me bad,
others held to be good.
And so it was wherever I went,
outlawed by all whom I met;
striving for gladness,
found only woe!
And so I was Wehwalt always;
Yes, Wehwalt! — sad was my fate.

Ein starkes Jagen auf uns
stellten die Neidinge an:
Der Jäger viele
fielen den Wölfen,
in Flucht durch den Wald
trieb sie das Wild:
wie Spreu zerstob uns der Feind.
Doch ward ich vom Vater versprengt;
seine Spur verlor ich,
je länger ich forschte:
eines Wolfes Fell nur
traf ich im Forst;
leer lag das vor mir,
[8] den Vater fand ich nicht.
Aus dem Wald trieb es mich fort;
[30b] mich drängt' es zu Männern und Frauen.
Wieviel ich traf
wo ich sie fand,
ob ich um Freund',
um Frauen warb,
immer doch war ich geächtet:
Unheil lag auf mir.
Was Rechtes je ich riet,
andern dünkte es arg,
was schlimm immer mir schien,
andere gaben ihm Gunst,
In Fehde fiel ich, wo ich mich fand,
Zorn traf mich, wohin ich zog;
gehrt' ich nach Wonne,
[5] weckt' ich nur Weh:
drum musst' ich mich Wehwalt nennen;
des Wehes waltet' ich nur.

59

(He turns his eyes to Sieglinde and observes her sympathetic glance.) [32, 30b, 5]

HUNDING

So the Norn who dealt you this fate,	Die so leidig Los dir beschied,
she felt no love for you:	nicht liebte dich die Norn':
no one greets you with joy	froh nicht grüsst dich der Mann,
when you arrive as guest.	dem fremd als Gast du nahst.

SIEGLINDE

Manly hearts do not fear	Feige nur fürchten den,
a weaponless lonely man!	[29] der waffenlos einsam fährt!
Tell us more, guest;	Künde noch, Gast,
tell of the fight	wie du im Kampf
in which your weapons were lost.	zuletzt die Waffe verlorst!

[31]

SIEGMUND
(with increasing excitement)

A girl in distress	Ein trauriges Kind
called for my aid;	rief mich zum Trutz:
her kinsman wanted	vermählen wollte
to force the maiden	der Magen Sippe
to marry a husband she feared.	dem Mann ohne Minne die Maid.
Hearing her cry,	Wider den Zwang
I came to her help.	zog ich zum Schutz,
Her cruel kin	der Dränger Tross
met me in fight;	traf ich im Kampf:
they fell before my spear.	dem Sieger sank der Feind.
I'd killed her fierce, cruel brothers.	Erschlagen lagen die Brüder:
The maid threw her arms round the dead;	die Leichen umschlang da die Maid,
her rage had turned into grief.	den Grimm verjagt' ihr der Gram.
With wildly streaming eyes	[5] Mit wilder Tränen Flut
she bathed the dead with her tears,	betroff sie weinend die Wal:
as she mourned for the death of those	um des Mordes der eignen Brüder
who'd wronged her — that ill-fated bride.	klagte die unsel'ge Braut.
Then her brothers' kinsmen	Der Erschlagnen Sippen
rushed to the fight;	stürmten daher;
vowing vengeance,	übermächtig
angrily fell on me,	ächzten nach Rache sie;
raging around me,	rings um die Stätte
eager to kill me.	ragten mir Feinde.
Meanwhile the maid	Doch von der Wal
stayed by the dead;	wich nicht die Maid;
my shield and spear	mit Schild und Speer
sheltered her life,	schirmt' ich sie lang,
till spear and shield	bis Speer und Schild
were hacked from my hand.	[28] im Harst mir zerhaun.
I was weaponless, wounded;	Wund und waffenlos stand ich —
she was killed while I watched:	sterben sah ich die Maid:
I fled from the furious host;	mich hetzte das wütende Heer —
on the bodies she lay dead.	[31] auf den Leichen lag sie tot.

(turning to Sieglinde with a look filled with sorrowful fervour)

You asked me, now you must know,	Nun weiss du, fragende Frau,
why I'm not Friedmund — but Wehwalt!	warum ich Friedmund — nicht heisse!

(He stands up and walks to the hearth. [33] *Sieglinde, pale and deeply stirred, lowers her eyes.)*

HUNDING
(rising)

I know a quarrelsome race;	Ich weiss ein wildes Geschlecht,
they do not respect	nicht heilig ist ihm,
what we revere;	was andern hehr:
they are hated by all men — and me.	[32] verhasst ist es allen und mir.
I heard a summons to vengeance:	Zur Rache ward ich gerufen,
death to the stranger	Sühne zu nehmen

who killed our kin!	für Sippenblut:
Too late came I,	zu spät kam ich
but now that I'm home,	und kehre nun heim,
I find that stranger here;	des flücht'gen Frevlers Spur
he sought my house for his rest.	im eignen Haus zu erspähn.

(He advances.)

My house guards you,	Mein Haus hütet,
Wölfing, today;	Wölfing, dich heut;
for the night you are my guest.	für die Nacht nahm ich dich auf;
But find some weapons [32]	mit starker Waffe
to serve you tomorrow;	doch wehre dich morgen;
I choose the day for our fight:	zum Kampfe kies ich den Tag:
you'll pay me blood for their blood.	für Tote zahlst du mir Zoll.

(With anxious gestures Sieglinde steps between the two men. Hunding, harshly:) [29]

Go from the room!	Fort aus dem Saal!
Why are you here!	Säume hier nicht!
Prepare my drink for the night,	Den Nachttrunk rüste mir drin
and wait for me in there.	und harre mein zur Ruh'.

[29]

(Sieglinde stands awhile undecided and thoughtful. Then she turns slowly and with hesitating steps towards the storeroom. There she again pauses and remains standing, lost in thought, with her face half turned away. With quiet resolve she opens the cupboard, fills a drinking horn, and shakes some spices into it from a container. Then she turns her eyes on Siegmund so as to meet his gaze, which he keeps unceasingly fixed on her. She perceives that Hunding is watching, and goes at once towards the bedchamber. On the steps she turns once more, looks yearningly at Siegmund, and indicates with her eyes, persistently and with eloquent earnestness, a particular spot in the ash-tree's trunk. [30a, 27] Hunding starts, and drives her with a violent gesture from the room. With a last look at Siegmund, she goes into the bedchamber, and closes the door behind her. Hunding takes down his weapons from the tree-trunk.) [32]

With weapons man should be armed.	Mit Waffen wahrt sich der Mann.

(to Siegmund, as he goes)

You, Wölfing, meet me tomorrow,	Dich, Wölfing, treffe ich morgen;
and then — fight with me!	mein Wort hörtest du —
Guard yourself well!	hüte dich wohl!

(He goes into the chamber; the closing of the bolt is heard from within.)

Scene Three. *Siegmund is alone. It has become quite dark. The room is lit only by a feeble fire on the hearth. Siegmund sinks down on the couch near the fire and broods silently for a while, in great agitation.* [32]

SIEGMUND

A sword was pledged by my father,	[27b]Ein Schwert verhiess mir der Vater,
to serve me in hour of need.	[32] ich fänd' es in höchster Not.
I am unarmed	Waffenlos fiel ich
in my enemy's house;	in Feindes Haus;
as a hostage here	seiner Rache Pfand,
helpless I wait.	raste ich hier.
But she's here too,	Ein Weib sah ich,
lovely and fair: [30b]	wonnig und hehr:
a new emotion	entzückend Bangen
fills my heart. [32]	zehrt mein Herz.
This woman who holds me bound,	Zu der mich nun Sehnsucht zieht,
whose enchantment tears at my heart,	die mit süssem Zauber mich sehrt,
as slave she's held by a man	im Zwange hält sie der Mann,
who mocks his weaponless foe.	der mich Wehrlosen höhnt!
Wälse! Wälse! [27b]	Wälse! Wälse!
Where is your sword?	Wo ist dein Schwert?
The shining sword	Das starke Schwert,
that alone can save me,	das im Sturm ich schwänge,
when there should break from my breast	bricht mir hervor aus der Brust,
that fury my heart still hides?	was wütend das Herz noch hegt?

(The fire collapses, and a bright glow springs up, striking the place on the ash-trunk indicated by Sieglinde's look, where now a sword-hilt is clearly seen.) [27]

What's glinting there	Was gleibt dort hell
to light the gloom?	im Glimmerschein?
On the ash-tree [27]	Welch ein Strahl bricht

there's a starry gleam.
My eyes are blinded,
dazzled with light;
lightnings flash from the tree.
  How the shining gleam
  inspires my heart!
  Is it the glance
  that shone from her eyes,
  did she leave it
  to linger behind,
when she was sent away?

aus der Esche Stamm?
Des Blinden Auge
leuchtet ein Blitz:
[27] lustig lacht da der Blick.
  Wie der Schein so hehr
  das Herz mir sengt!
  Ist es der Blick
  der blühenden Frau,
  den dort haftend
  sie hinter sich liess,
als aus dem Saal sie schied?

(From now on, the fire on the hearth gradually sinks.)

Shadows of darkness
covered my eyes;
but her radiant glance
fell on me then,
warming and lighting my heart.
  Glorious rays
  of the golden sun,
  with gladdening splendour
  encircled my head,
till in the mountains it sank.

Nächtiges Dunkel
deckte mein Aug';
ihres Blickes Strahl
streifte mich da:
Wärme gewann ich und Tag.
  Selig schien mir
  der Sonne Licht;
  den Scheitel umgliss mir
  ihr wonniger Glanz,
bis hinter Bergen sie sank.

(a new faint gleam from the fire)

Yet once more, as it went,
evening radiance did shine;
and the ancient ash-tree's trunk
was bathed in a golden glow;
  that light is fading;
  the gleam has gone;
  shadows of darkness
  gather around me:
deep in my breast there lingers on
that last smouldering glow.

Noch einmal, da sie schied,
traf mich abends ihr Schein;
selbst der alten Esche Stamm
[27] erglänzte in goldner Glut:
  da bleicht die Blüte,
  das Licht verlischt;
  nächtiges Dunkel
  deckt mir das Auge:
tief in des Busens Berge
[32] glimmt nur noch lichtlose Glut.

(The fire has burnt out; complete darkness. The door at the side opens softly. Sieglinde, in a white garment, comes out and advances lightly but quickly towards the hearth.)

SIEGLINDE

Are you awake?

Schläfst du, Gast?

SIEGMUND
(springing up in joyful surprise)

Who steals this way?

Wer schleicht daher?

SIEGLINDE

I do. Listen to me!
In heavy sleep lies Hunding;
I gave him a drug in his drink,
Now, in the night, you are safe!

Ich bin's: höre mich an!
In tiefem Schlaf liegt Hunding;
ich würzt' ihm betäubenden Trank:
Nütze die Nacht dir zum Heil!

SIEGMUND
(interrupting her passionately)

Safe when you are near!

Heil macht mich dein Nah'n!

SIEGLINDE

There's a sword for him who can win it;
and when that sword is won,
  then I can call you
  noblest of heroes:
  the strongest alone
  masters the sword.
So listen well, mark what I tell you!
  My husband's kinsmen
  sat in this room,
they'd come here to witness his wedding.
  He married a wife
  against her will;

Eine Waffe lass mich dir weisen:
O wenn du sie gewännst!
  Den hehrsten Helden
  dürft' ich dich heissen:
  dem Stärksten allein
[27] ward sie bestimmt.
O merke wohl, was ich dir melde!
  Der Männer Sippe
  sass hier im Saal,
von Hunding zur Hochzeit geladen.
  Er freite ein Weib,
  das ungefragt

robbers had made her their prize.
  Sadly, I sat here
  while they were drinking;
a stranger entered this house:
an old man dressed all in grey;
his hat hung so low
that one of his eyes was hidden;
  but the other's flash
  filled them with terror:
  none could counter
  that threatening gaze.
  I alone
  felt in those glances
sweet, yearning regret —
sorrow and solace in one.
  On me smiling,
  he glared at the others;
in his hand he carried a sword;
  then drove it deep
  in the ash-tree's trunk;
to the hilt buried it there.
But one man alone could win it,
he who could draw it forth.
  The guests were warriors;
  they rose to the challenge;
but none could master the sword.
  Many tried it
  but all were baffled;
  the strongest seized it in vain —
none could move the blade from its place.
That sword is still in the tree.
I knew then who he was,
come to greet me in my grief;
  I know too
  who alone
can draw the sword from the tree.
  And oh, have I found
  today that friend,
  come from the distance
  to end my grief?
  Then all I have suffered
  in pain and distress,
  yes, all I have suffered
  in sorrow and shame,
  all is forgotten,
  all is atoned for!
  Regained all things
  I thought I had lost;
  my fondest desires
  gain their fulfilment,
if I have found that friend,
and hold that hero to me!

Schächer ihm schenkten zur Frau.
  Traurig sass ich,
  während sie tranken;
[8] ein Fremder trat da herein:
ein Greis in grauem Gewand;
tief hing ihm der Hut,
der deckt' ihm der Augen eines;
  doch des andren Strahl,
  Angst schuf er allen,
  traf die Männer
  sein mächt'ges Dräu'n:
  Mir allein
  weckte das Auge
süss sehnenden Harm,
[27] Tränen und Trost zugleich.
  Auf mich blickt' er
  und blitzte auf jene,
als ein Schwert in Händen er schwang;
  das stiess er nun
  in der Esche Stamm,
bis zum Heft haftet' es drin:
dem sollte der Stahl geziemen,
der aus dem Stamm es zög'.
  Der Männer alle,
  so kühn sie sich mühten,
die Wehr sich keiner gewann;
  Gäste kamen
  und Gäste gingen,
  die stärksten zogen am Stahl —
[27] keinen Zoll entwich er dem Stamm:
dort haftet schweigend das Schwert.
[8] Da wusst' ich, wer der war,
der mich Gramvolle gegrüsst;
  ich weiss auch,
  wem allein
[27] im Stamm das Schwert er bestimmt.
  O fänd' ich ihn heut
  und hier, den Freund;
  käm' er aus Fremden
  zur ärmsten Frau:
  Was je ich gelitten
  in grimmigem Leid,
  was je mich geschmerzt
  in Schande und Schmach —
  süsseste Rache
  sühnte dann alles!
  Erjagt hätt' ich,
  was je ich verlor,
  was je ich beweint,
  wär' mir gewonnen,
fänd' ich den heiligen Freund,
umfing' den Helden mein Arm!

SIEGMUND
(embracing Sieglinde with ardour) [33]

Yes, loveliest bride,
I am that friend;
both weapon and wife I claim!
  Fierce in my breast
  blazes the vow
that binds me ever to you.
  For all that I've sought
  I see now in you;
  in you, all things
  I longed for are found.
  Though you were shamed,

Dich, selige Frau,
hält nun der Freund,
dem Waffe und Weib bestimmt!
  Heiss in der Brust
  brennt mir der Eid,
der mich dir Edlen vermählt.
  Was je ich ersehnt,
  ersah ich in dir;
  in dir fand ich,
  was je mir gefehlt!
  Littest du Schmach,

though sad was my life,	und schmerzte mich Leid;
though I was outlawed,	war ich geächtet,
and you were disgraced,	und warst du entehrt:
joyful vengeance	freudige Rache
calls us to gladness!	ruft nun den Frohen!
I laugh now	Auf lach ich
in fullest delight,	in heiliger Lust —
as I embrace your glory,	halt ich die Hehre umfangen,
feel your beating heart!	fühl ich dein schlagendes Herz!

(The large door flies open.)

SIEGLINDE
(starts in alarm, and tears herself away.)

Ah, who went? Or who has come?	Ha, wer ging? Wer kam herein?

(The door remains open; outside, a glorious spring night; the full moon shines in, throwing its bright light on the pair; so that suddenly they can fully and clearly see each other.)

SIEGMUND
(in gentle ecstasy)

No one went —	Keiner ging,
but one has come:	doch einer kam:
see him, the Spring	siehe, der Lenz
smiles on our love!	lacht in den Saal!

(Siegmund draws Sieglinde to him on the couch with tender vehemence, so that she sits beside him. Increasing brilliance of the moonlight.)

Winter storms have vanished	Winterstürme wichen
at Spring's command;	dem Wonnemond,
in gentle radiance	in mildem Lichte
sparkles the Spring,	leuchtet der Lenz;
on balmy breezes,	auf linden Lüften
light and lovely,	leicht und lieblich,
working wonders	Wunder webend
on his way;	er sich wiegt:
on wood and meadow	durch Wald und Auen
softly breathing;	weht sein Atem,
wide and smiling	weit geöffnet
are his eyes.	lach sein Aug'.
The songs of happy birds	Aus sel'ger Vöglein Sange
reflect his voice;	süss er tönt,
sweet the fragrance	holde Düfte
of his breath;	haucht er aus:
from his ardent blood the flowers	seinem warmen Blut entblühen
are joyfully blooming;	wonnige Blumen,
buds and blooms	Keim und Spross
have sprung at his call.	entspringt seiner Kraft.
He waves his wand of magic	Mit zarter Waffen Zier
over the world;	bezwingt er die Welt;
winter and storm yield	Winter und Sturm wichen
to his strong command:	der starken Wehr:
as soon as his word was spoken	Wohl musste den tapfern Streichen
the doors that barred him were broken,	die strenge Türe auch weichen,
for how could they keep us	die trotzig und starr
parted from him?	uns — trennte von ihm.
To clasp his sister	Zu seiner Schwester
here he has flown;	schwang er sich her;
for Love called to the Spring;	die Liebe lockte den Lenz:
and Love lay hidden	in unsrem Busen
deep in our hearts;	barg sie sich tief;
but now she laughs to the light.	nun lacht sie selig dem Licht.
The bride and sister	Die bräutliche Schwester
is freed by her brother;	befreite der Bruder;
the barriers fall	zertrümmert liegt,
that held them apart;	was sie je getrennt;
joyful greeting	jauchzend grüsst sich
as now they meet:	das junge Paar:
united are Love and Spring!	vereint sind Liebe und Lenz!

The markers [30b] and [30a] appear in the left margin between the columns at the lines "parted from him?" / "uns — trennte von ihm." and "To clasp his sister" / "Zu seiner Schwester".

You are the Spring,
  that Spring I have yearned for
in frost and in winter's ice.
  My heart felt the spell,
  grew warm when you came;
when my eyes beheld you, I knew you.
Everything used to be strange,
friendless all that was round me;
like far off things and unknown,
all that ever drew near.
  But you came
and all was clear:
for I knew you were mine
when I beheld you.
What I hid in my heart,
all I am,
bright as the day,
all was revealed;
the sound of this truth
rang in my ear,
when in winter's frosty desert
my eyes first beheld my friend.

[30a] Du bist der Lenz,
  nach dem ich verlangte
in frostigen Winters Frist.
  Dich grüsste mein Herz
  mit heiligem Grau'n,
als dein Blick zuerst mir erblühte.
Fremdes nur sah ich von je,
freundlos war mir das Nahe;
als hätt' ich nie es gekannt,
war, was immer mir kam.
[30b] Doch dich kannt' ich
deutlich und klar:
als mein Auge dich sah,
warst du mein Eigen:
was im Busen ich barg,
was ich bin,
hell wie der Tag
taucht' es mir auf,
wie tönender Schall
schlug's an mein Ohr,
als in frostig öder Fremde
zuerst ich den Freund ersah.

(She throws her arms around his neck, enraptured, and gazes closely into his face.)

SIEGMUND
(carried away)

Oh sweetest enchantment,
woman most blessed!

O süsseste Wonne!
Seligstes Weib!

SIEGLINDE
(close to his eyes) [11a]

Oh hold me near you,
and clasp me to you,
to see more clearly
that holy light
that shines from eyes,
from countenance,
and so sweetly steals to my heart.

O lass in Nähe
zu dir mich neigen
dass hell ich schaue
den hehren Schein,
der dir aus Aug'
[30b] und Antlitz bricht
und so süss die Sinne mir zwingt.

SIEGMUND

The Spring's fair moon
shines on you here,
crowns with glory
your lovely hair.
Ah, now I know
what captured my heart;
my glances feast in delight.

Im Lenzesmond
leuchtest du hell;
hehr umwebt dich
das Wellenhaar:
Was mich berückt,
errat ich nun leicht —
denn wonnig weidet mein Blick.

SIEGLINDE
(pushes the locks back from his brow, and gazes at him in astonishment.)

Your noble brow
is broad and clear;
its delicate veins
with my fingers I trace!
I tremble with the rapture
of my delight!
A marvel stirs in my memory:
although you came but today,
I've seen your face before!

Wie dir die Stirn
so offen steht,
der Adern Geäst
in den Schläfen sich schlingt!
[8] Mir zagt es vor der Wonne,
die mich entzückt!
Ein Wunder will mich gemahnen:
den heut zuerst ich erschaut,
mein Auge sah dich schon!

SIEGMUND

I know your dream,
I feel it too:
in ardent yearning
you were my dream!

Ein Minnetraum
gemahnt auch mich:
in heissem Sehnen
sah ich dich schon!

The stream has shown
my reflected face —
and now I find it before me;
in you I see it again,
just as it shone from the stream!

Im Bach erblickt' ich
mein eigen Bild —
und jetzt gewahr ich es wieder:
wie einst dem Teich es enttaucht,
bietest mein Bild mir nun du!

SIEGMUND

Yours is the face
that I knew in my heart.

[30a] Du bist das Bild,
das ich in mir barg.

SIEGLINDE
(*quickly turning her eyes away from him*)

Be still! Again
that voice is sounding,
the voice that I heard
once as a child —
But no! I know when I heard it:

O still! Lass mich
der Stimme lauschen:
mich dünkt, ihren Klang
hört' ich als Kind —
Doch nein, ich hörte sie neulich,
(*excitedly*)

when through the woods I called,
and echo called in reply.

als meiner Stimme Schall
mir widerhallte der Wald.

SIEGMUND

Oh loveliest music,
voice that I longed for!

O lieblichste Laute,
denen ich lausche!

SIEGLINDE
(*again gazing into his eyes*) [33, 27]

And your gleaming glance,
I've seen it before:
the stranger in grey
gazed on me thus
when he came to console my grief.
By that glance
his child knew him well —
I knew by what name I should call him!

Deines Auges Glut
erglänzte mir schon:
so blickte der Greis
grüssend auf mich,
als der Traurigen Trost er gab.
An dem Blick
erkannt' ihn sein Kind —
schon wollt' ich beim Namen ihn nennen!

[8]

(*She pauses for a moment and then continues softly.*)
Wehwalt, is that what you're called?

Wehwalt heisst du fürwahr?

SIEGMUND

No more that name,
now you are mine:
my sorrow has turned to gladness!

Nicht heiss ich so,
seit du mich liebst:
nun walt ich der hehrsten Wonnen!

SIEGLINDE

And Friedmund was no name
for a sufferer.

Und Friedmund darfst du
froh dich nicht nennen?

SIEGMUND

Name me yourself;
by what name can you love me?
My name, I take it from you!

Nenne mich du,
wie du liebst, dass ich heisse:
den Namen nehm ich von dir!

SIEGLINDE

You told me that Wolf was your father.

Doch nanntest du Wolfe den Vater?

SIEGMUND

A Wolf when he hunted foxes!
But when his eye
shone on me proudly,
as your eyes shine on me now,
why then — Wälse his name.

Ein Wolf war er feigen Füchsen!
Doch dem so stolz
strahlte das Auge,
wie, Herrliche, hehr dir es strahlt,
der war: Wälse genannt.

SIEGLINDE
(*beside herself*)

Was Wälse your father,

War Wälse dein Vater

and are you a Wälsung?	und bist du ein Wälsung,
Then it is yours,	stiess er für dich
that sword in the tree!	sein Schwert in den Stamm —
So now let me name you	so lass mich dich heissen
as I have loved you:	wie ich dich liebe:
Siegmund —	Siegmund —
that is your name!	so nenn ich dich!

SIEGMUND
(*He leaps up, hurries to the trunk, and grasps the sword hilt.*) [33]

Siegmund call me,		Siegmund heiss ich
and Siegmund am I!	[27]	und Siegmund bin ich!
The proof is the sword,		Bezeug' es dies Schwert,
my hand soon shall hold it!		das zaglos ich halte!
Promised by Wälse	[9]	Wälse verhiess mir,
in hour of need,		in höchster Not
now it is found;		fänd' ich es einst:
I grasp it now!		ich fass es nun!
Holiest love	[7]	Heiligster Minne
in highest need,		höchste Not,
yearning desire		sehnender Liebe
in longing and need,		sehrende Not
burning bright in my breast,		brennt mir hell in der Brust,
drives to deeds and death.		drängst zu Tat und Tod:
Notung! Notung!	[27b]	Notung! Notung!
So name I the sword!		So nenn ich dich, Schwert.
Notung! Notung!		Notung! Notung!
Bright, shining steel!		Neidlicher Stahl!
Show me your sharpness,		Zeig deiner Schärfe
glorious blade!		schneidenden Zahn:
Come forth from the scabbard to me!		heraus aus der Scheide zu mir!

(*With a powerful effort, Siegmund draws the sword from the tree, and shows it to the astonished and enraptured Sieglinde.*) [27]

Siegmund, the Wälsung,		Siegmund, den Wälsung,
here you see!	[33]	siehst du, Weib!
As bride-gift		Als Brautgabe
he brings you this sword:		bringt er dies Schwert:
he claims with it		so freit er sich
his loveliest bride;		die seligste Frau;
and from this house		dem Feindeshaus
he leads her away.		entführt er dich so.
Far from here,		Fern von hier
follow me now,		folge mir nun,
forth to the laughing	[27]	fort in des Lenzes
land of bright Spring.		lachendes Haus:
Your guard is Notung, the sword,	[30b]	dort schützt dich Notung, das Schwert,
should Siegmund die, conquered by love!		wenn Siegmund dir liebend erlag!

(*He has embraced her, to draw her away with him.*)

SIEGLINDE
(*In highest excitement she tears herself away, and stands before him.*)

Is this Siegmund,	Bist du Siegmund,
standing before me?	den ich hier sehe —
Sieglinde am I;	Sieglinde bin ich,
I longed for you.	die dich ersehnt:
Your own dear sister	Die eigne Schwester
and bride you have won with the sword!	gewannst du zu eins mit dem Schwert!

SIEGMUND [30b]

Bride and sister		Braut und Schwester
be to your brother;		bist du dem Bruder —
the blood of the Wälsungs is blessed!	[27]	so blühe denn, Wälsungenblut!

(*He draws her to him with passionate fervour; with a cry, she falls on his breast. The curtain falls quickly.*) [30a]

Act Two

A wild, craggy place. In the background, a gorge slopes up from below to a high ridge of rocks, from which the ground again sinks to the front.

Scene One. *Wotan, armed for battle, carrying his spear; before him Brünnhilde, as a Valkyrie, likewise fully armed.* [27, 11b/30a, 34]

WOTAN

Go bridle your horse,		Nun zäume dein Ross
warrior maid!		reisige Maid!
Seize your shield;		Bald entbrennt
battle is near.	[9]	brünstiger Streit:
Brünnhilde's off to the fight,		Brünnhilde stürme zum Kampf,
the Wälsung is victor today!		dem Wälsung kiese sie Sieg!
Hunding falls to him;		Hunding wähle sich,
leave him to lie;		wem er gehört;
for Walhall he is not fit.		nach Walhall taugt er mir nicht.
So hasten away,		Drum rustig und rasch
ride to the field!		reite zur Wal!

BRÜNNHILDE
(shouting as she leaps from rock to rock up to the heights on the right)

Hoyotoho! Hoyotoho!	[34, 35]	Hojotoho! Hojotoho!
Hiaha! Hiaha!		Heiaha! Heiaha!
Hoyotoyo! Hiaha!		Hojotoho! Heiaha!

(On a high peak she stops, looks into the gorge at the back, and calls to Wotan.)

I warn you, father,		Dir rat ich, Vater,
look to yourself;		rüste dich selbst;
brave the storm		harten Sturm
blowing your way.		sollst du bestehn.
Fricka's coming — your wife;		Fricka naht, deine Frau,
she's drawn along by two of her rams.		im Wagen mit dem Widdergespann.
Hi! How she swings	[5]	Hei, wie die goldne
her glittering whip!		Geissel sie schwingt!
The wretched beasts		Die armen Tiere
are sweating with fear;		ächzen vor Angst;
wheels rattle and rumble,		wild rasseln die Räder;
whirl her on to the fray.		zornig fährt sie zum Zank!
A woman's battle		In solchem Strausse
is not to my taste,		streit ich nicht gern,
rather the clangour		lieb ich auch mutiger
of martial arms.	[34]	Männer Schlacht.
Be sure that you weather the storm;		Drum sieh, wie den Sturm du bestehst:
I'm happy to leave it to you!		ich Lustige lass dich im Stich!
Hoyotoho! Hoyotoho!	[35]	Hojotoho! Hojotoho!
Hiaha! Hiaha!		Heiaha! Heiaha!
Hiahaha!		Heiahaha!

(Brünnhilde disappears behind the mountain height at the side. Fricka, in a chariot drawn by two rams, comes up from the gorge to the top of the rocky ridge, where she stops suddenly and alights. She strides impetuously towards Wotan in the foreground.)

WOTAN
(seeing Fricka approaching; aside)

The usual storm,	Der alte Sturm,
the usual strife!	die alte Müh'!
But here I must be steadfast!	Doch stand muss ich hier halten!

FRICKA
(as she approaches, moderates her pace and places herself with dignity before Wotan.)

In the mountains where you hide,	Wo in den Bergen du dich birgst,
to shun the sight of your wife,	der Gattin Blick zu entgehn,

here I have found you at last, to claim the help that you owe me.	einsam hier such ich dich auf, dass Hilfe du mir verhiessest.

WOTAN

Let Fricka's troubles freely be told.	Was Fricka kümmert, künde sie frei.

[32]

FRICKA

I have heard Hunding's cry:
revenge the wrong they have done!
    As wedlock's guardian
    I answered him.
    I swore
I would punish the deed
this pair dared to commit,
who wronged a husband and me.
	Ich vernahm Hundings Not,
	um Rache rief er mich an:
	    der Ehe Hüterin
	    hörte ihn,
	    verhiess streng
	zu strafen die Tat
	des frech frevelnden Paars,
	das kühn den Gatten gekränkt.

WOTAN

But what evil
have they done?
The Spring enticed them to love.
    The power of love
    overcame them both;
and who can resist that power?
	Was so Schlimmes
	schuf das Paar,
	[30b]das liebend einte der Lenz?
	    Der Minne Zauber
	    entzückte sie:
	wer büsst mir der Minne Macht?

FRICKA

Pretend that you don't understand!
And yet you know all too well,
    that I have come
    to avenge marriage vows,
the holy vows they have broken!
	* Wie töricht und taub du dich stellst,
	als wüsstest fürwahr du nicht,
	    dass um der Ehe
	    heiligen Eid,
	den hart gekränkten, ich klage!

WOTAN

Unholy call I the vows that bind unloving hearts;	Unheilig acht ich den Eid der Unliebende eint;

---

* Wagner originally wrote the following longer text for this scene which he discarded when he came to set it to music. He retained it as a footnote to his edition of the Collected Works.

FRICKA

Pretend that you don't understand,
and yet you know all too well,
    what crime it is that
    Fricka complains of,
that distresses her heart.
	Wie töricht und taub du dich sellst,
	als wüsstest fürwahr du nicht
	    an welchen Frevel
	    Fricka dich mahnt,
	was im Herzen sie härmt.

WOTAN

You see only one thing, while I see another that chases the first from my sight.	Du siehst nur das Eine; das Andre seh ich, das Jenes mir jagt aus dem Blick.

FRICKA

I see just that one thing
I must always protect:
the holy marriage vow.
    My soul rejects
    him who harms it;
he who spoils it, strikes at my heart.
	Das Eine nur seh ich,
	was ewig ich hüte,
	der Ehe heiligen Eid:
	    meine Seele kränkt
	    wer ihn versehrt,
	wer ihn trübt, trifft mir das Herz.

WOTAN

You speak with confidence of marriage,	So zweifellos sprichst du von Ehe,

69

and do you
expect me to act,
to exert my power
where yours is helpless?
For where bold spirits are moving,
I stir them ever to strife.

und mir wahrlich
mute nicht zu,
dass mit Zwang ich halte,
[9] was dir nicht haftet:
denn wo kühn Kräfte sich regen,
da rat ich offen zum Krieg.

FRICKA

If you encourage
adulterous love,
then proudly go further
and praise as holy
the incest there has been —
the love of a pair of twins!
My senses are shocked,
my mind is amazed —
bridal embrace
of sister and brother!
When came it to pass
that brother and sister were lovers?

Achtest du rühmlich
der Ehe Bruch,
so prahle nun weiter
und preis es heilig,
dass Blutschande entblüht
dem Bund eines Zwillingspaars!
Mir schaudert das Herz,
es schwindelt mein Hirn:
bräutlich umfing
die Schwester der Bruder!
Wann ward es erlebt,
dass leiblich Geschwister sich liebten?

where I see the power of love.
Unholy
I call the vow
that binds unloving hearts.
Less harshly
you'd judge that wife
if yourself you'd felt the force
by which Hunding won his bride.

wo nur Zwang der Liebe ich seh?
Unheilig
acht ich den Eid,
der Unliebende eint.
Wahrlich, leicht
wiegt dir das Weib,
weihest du selbst die Gewalt,
die für Hunding freite Frau!

FRICKA

When blind aggression,
unchecked and wild,
seeks to shatter the world,
who alone upholds
disaster's cause
but Wotan the wrathful one?
Weakness you never shield,
strength alone you guard;
the rage of humans
in rough actions,
murder, pillage
are your achievements,
while mine is only to retain
that one thing holy and sublime.
Wherever peace
is found in conflict;
wherever change
gives to valour
a more gentle aspect —
there I listen for its voice.
The breaks in morality's
guiding line
I fasten again:
where all has been lost,
I refresh myself
in the holy dew of hope.
If once Hunding
practised the power
I through weakness no longer wielded,
you allowed the use of violence;
when he atoned
for his crime and guilt,
a friend he found in Fricka,
through his holy marriage vow.

Wenn blinde Gewalt
trotzig und wild
rings zertrümmert die Welt,
wer trägt einzig
des Unheils Schuld,
als Wotan, Wütender, du?
Schwache beschirmst du nie,
Starken stehst du nur bei:
der Männer Rasen
in rauhem Mut,
Mord und Raub
ist dein mächtig Werk;
das meine doch ist es allein,
dass Eines noch heilig und hehr.
Wo nach Ruhe
der Rauhe sich sehnt,
wo des Wechsels
sehrender Wut
wehre sanft ein Besitz, —
dort steh ich lauschend still.
Der zerrissenen Sitte
lenkendes Seil
bind ich neü zum Band:
wo Alles verloren,
lab ich mich so
an der Hoffnung heiligem Tau.
Übte Hunding
einstens Gewalt,
was ich Schwache nicht wehren konnte,
du liessest es kühn gewahren:
sühnte er dann
des Frevels Schuld,
Freundin ward ihm da Fricka
durch heiliger Ehe Eid:

Now it's come to pass!	Heut — hast du's erlebt!
And learn from this	Erfahre so,
that a thing may happen	was von selbst sich fügt,
although it's not happened before.	[30b] sei zuvor auch noch nie es geschehn.
They love one another,	Das jene sich lieben,
as you must know;	leuchtet dir hell;
so hear my words of advice:	drum höre redlichen Rat:
since Fricka is famed	Soll süsse Lust
for her blessing on lovers,	deinen Segen dir lohnen,
bestow on them your blessing,	so segne, lachend der Liebe,
on Siegmund's and Sieglinde's love!	Siegmunds und Sieglindes Bund!

So I forget	so vergess ich
his old transgression;	was je er beging,
with my protection	mit meinem Schutze
I shield his rights:	schirm' ich sein Recht.
one who discontinues his crime,	Der nicht seinem Frevel gesteuert,
no longer opposes my peace.	meinen Frieden stör' er nun nicht!

WOTAN

Did I oppose	Stört' ich dich je
your rightful power?	in deinem Walten?
Always I let you wield it.	Gewähren liess ich dich stets.
Tying together with	Knüpfe du bindender
binding knots,	Knoten Band,
fetters those who won't be bound;	fessle was nicht sich fügt;
pretend there's peace	heuchle Frieden,
and nobly rejoice	und freue dich hehr
over lying vows of love;	ob gelogner Liebe Eid:
but don't expect	doch mir, wahrlich,
me to feel obliged	mute nicht zu,
to exert my power	dass mit Zwang ich halte
where yours is helpless.	was dir nich haftet;
For where bold spirits are stirring,	denn wo kühn Kräfte sich regen,
I often allow them to fight.	da gewähr' ich offen dem Krieg.

† **FRICKA**

If you encourage	Achtest du rühmlich
adulterous love,	der Ehe Bruch,
then proudly go further	so prahle nun weiter
and praise as holy	und preis es heilig,
the incest there has been —	dass Blutschande entblüht
the love of a pair of twins!	dem Bund eines Zwillingspaars.
My senses are shocked,	Mir schaudert das Herz,
my mind is amazed —	es schwindelt mein Hirn:
bridal embrace	bräutlich umfing
of sister and brother!	die Schwester der Bruder!
When came it to pass	Wann — ward es erlebt,
that brother and sister were lovers?	dass leiblich Geschwister sich liebten?

† **WOTAN**

Now it's come to pass!	Heut — hast du's erlebt:
And learn from this	erfahre so
that a thing may happen	was von selbst sich fügt,
although it's not happened before.	sei zuvor auch nie es geschehn.

FRICKA

Is your contempt	So frechen Hohn
all my grief arouses?	nur weckt dir mein Harm?
Is your scorn all I deserve	Deinen Spott nur erzielt
for my burning rage?	mein brennender Zorn?
Do you deride the dignity	Verlachst du die Würde,
you yourself bestowed?	die selbst du verliehn?

FRICKA
(breaking out in deep indignation)

So this is the end
of the gods and their glory,
now you have fathered
Wölfing the Wälsung?
I speak frankly;
am I not right?
The race of the gods
by you is forgotten!
You cast aside
what you once held in honour;
you break every bond
that you tied to unite us;
loosen, laughing,
your hold on heaven: [27]
that the lustful lovers may flourish,
this sinful incestuous pair,
who were born as the fruit of your shame!
Oh, why mourn [17]
over virtue and vows, [30a]
when first they were broken by you!
Your faithful wife
you've always betrayed;
down in the caverns,
high on the mountains,
your glance searched
and lusted for love,
where your roving fancy might lead you.
Your scorn has broken my heart.
Sad in my spirit,
I had to see you

So ist es denn aus
mit den ewigen Göttern,
seit du die wilden
Wälsungen zeugtest?
Heraus sagt' ich's;
traf ich den Sinn?
Nichts gilt dir der Hehren
heilige Sippe;
hin wirfst du alles,
was einst du geachtet;
zerreissest die Bande,
die selbst du gebunden,
lösest lachend
des Himmels Haft:
dass nach Lust und Laune nur walte
dies frevelnde Zwillingspaar,
deiner Untreue zuchtlose Frucht!
O, was klag ich
um Ehe und Eid,
da zuerst du selbst sie versehrt.
Die treue Gattin
trogest du stets;
wo eine Tiefe,
wo eine Höhe,
dahin lugte
lüstern dein Blick,
wie des Wechsels Lust du gewännst
und höhnend kränktest mein Herz.
Trauernden Sinnes
musst' ich's ertragen,

Do you crush the honour
of your own wife?
Where are you storming,
furious god,
will you destroy the world
to which you gave law and order?

Zertrittst du die Ehre
des eignen Weibes?
Wohin rennst du,
rasender Gott,
reissest der Schöpfung du ein,
der selbst das Gesetz du gabst?

WOTAN

By primal law
I govern all men;
where the strong are born and flourish,
I build my sphere of action;
wherever it flows,
I guide that stream,
shielding the source
from which it springs.
Where life and love are strong,
I protect that vital force.
The pair of twins
conquered my power;
love was fostered
in their mother's womb;
instinctively it lay there once,
instinctively it is cherished now.
Should a sweeter reward
with your blessing flourish,
then divine, holy
favour will bless
Siegmund's and Sieglinde's love.

Des Urgesetzes
walt ich vor Allem:
wo Kräfte zeugen und kreisen,
zieh ich meines Wirkens Kreis;
wohin er läuft
leit ich den Strom,
den Quell hüt ich
aus dem er quillt:
wo Liebes- und Liebeskraft,
da wahrt ich mir Lebensmacht.
Das Zwillingspaar
zwang meine Macht:
Minne nährt' es
im Mutterschooss;
unbewusst las es einst dort,
unbewusst liebt es sich jetzt.
Soll süsser Lohn
deinem Segen entblühn
so segne mit göttlich
heiliger Gunst
Siegmunds und Sieglindes Bund.

* translated by Elizabeth Forbes, except for the two speeches marked † which are part of
Andrew Porter's translation of the final text. The original text continues with Fricka's
speech at the top of this page.

leading to battle	zogst du zur Schlacht
those barbarous maidens	mit den schlimmen Mädchen,
your lawless love	die wilder Minne
had brought into being;	Bund dir gebar:
but you still respected your wife,	denn dein Weib noch scheutest du so.
for the Valkyrie brood,	dass der Walküren Schar
and Brünnhild herself	und Brünnhilde selbst,
whom you loved so well —	deines Wunsches Braut,
they were bound in obedience to me.	in Gehorsam der Herrin du gabst.
But now a new name	Doch jetzt, da dir neue
has taken your fancy,	Namen gefielen,
and 'Wälse' prowls	als 'Wälse' wölfisch
like a wolf through the woodland;	im Walde du schweiftest;
now you have stooped	jetzt, da zu niedrigster
to the depth of dishonour,	Schmach du dich neigtest,
a common woman	gemeiner Menschen
has borne you her children:	ein Paar zu erzeugen:
now to whelps of a she-wolf	jetzt dem Wurfe der Wölfin
you would abandon your wife!	wirfst du zu Füssen dein Weib!
Go on with your work!	So führ es denn aus!
Fill now my cup!	Fülle das Mass!
You betrayed me; let me be trampled!	Die Betrogne lass auch zertreten!

WOTAN
(*quietly*)

You never learn	Nichts lerntest du,
what I would teach you,	wollt' ich dich lehren,
to try to conceive a deed	was nie du erkennen kannst,
before that deed comes to pass.	eh' nicht ertagte die Tat.
Your concern	Stets Gewohntes
is for things that have been;	nur magst du verstehn:
but what is still to come —	doch was noch nie sich traf,
to that turn all my thoughts.	[27] danach trachtet mein Sinn.
Hear this one thing!	Eines höre!
We need a man	Not tut ein Held,
who lives without our protection,	der, leidig göttlichen Schutzes,
who is free from the rule of the gods.	[9] sich löse vom Göttergesetz.
He alone	So nur taugt er
can accomplish the deed,	zu wirken die Tat,
which, although it will save us,	[6] die, wie not sie den Göttern,
the gods are forbidden to do.	dem Gott doch zu wirken verwehrt.
[15]	

FRICKA

With crafty reasoning	Mit tiefem Sinne
you would deceive me.	willst du mich täuschen:
What marvel can be worked	was Hehres sollten
by these mortals?	Helden je wirken,
What is this deed which gods cannot do?	das ihren Göttern wäre verwehrt,
And who gives the mortals their power?	deren Gunst in ihnen nur wirkt?

WOTAN

Do you rate their own	Ihres eignen Mutes
achievement so low?	achtest du nicht?

FRICKA

Who breathed the soul into men?	Wer hauchte Menschen ihn ein?
Who kindled the light in their eyes?	Wer hellte den Blöden den Blick?
When you are near,	In deinem Schutz
then they are strong;	scheinen sie stark,
when you inspire them,	durch deinen Stachel
then they can strive.	streben sie auf:
You fill them with daring,	du reizest sie einzig,
then sing their praises to me.	die so mir Ew'gen du rühmst.
With new deceits	Mit neuer List
you are trying to trick me;	willst du mich belügen,

73

with new excuses
you would escape me;
but for this Wälsung
you plead all in vain;
in him I find only you;
what he does, he does through you.

durch neue Ränke
mir jetzt entrinnen;
doch diesen Wälsung
gewinnst du dir nicht:
in ihm treff ich nur dich,
denn durch dich trotzt er allein.

WOTAN
(*with emotion*)

In wildest sorrow
he grew by himself;
and I gave him no help.

[9]   In wildem Leiden
erwuchs er sich selbst:
mein Schutz schirmte ihn nie.

FRICKA

Then do not help him now!
Take back the sword
you placed in his hand.

So schütz auch heut ihn nicht!
Nimm ihm das Schwert,
[27]   das du ihm geschenkt!

WOTAN

The sword?

Das Schwert?

FRICKA

Yes, the sword,
the magical,
glittering sword,
that the god has given his son!

Ja, das Schwert,
das zauberstark
zuckende Schwert,
das du Gott dem Sohne gabst.

WOTAN
(*violently*)

Siegmund has won it himself
(*with a suppressed shudder*)
in his need.

Siegmund gewann es sich
selbst in der Not.

(*From this point, Wotan's whole demeanour expresses an ever-increasingly uneasy, profound dejection.*) [36]

FRICKA
(*continuing eagerly*)

You sent him the need,
as you sent him the sword.
Can you deceive me,
when day and night
I have watched every step?
For him you prepared
that sword in the tree,
and you promised him
it would be found.
Can you deny it,
that your hand alone
has led him where it was found?

Du schufst ihm die Not
wie das neidliche Schwert.
Willst du mich täuschen,
die Tag und Nacht
auf den Fersen dir folgt?
Für ihn stiessest du
das Schwert in den Stamm,
du verhiessest ihm
die hehre Wehr:
willst du es leugnen,
dass nur deine List
ihn lockte, wo er es fänd'?

(*Wotan makes a wrathful gesture. Fricka becomes ever more confident, as she sees the impression she has made on Wotan.*)

With bondsmen
the gods do not battle;
rebellious slaves must be punished.
As an equal
I argue with you;
but Siegmund I claim as my slave.

Mit Unfreien
streitet kein Edler,
den Frevler straft nur der Freie.
Wider deine Kraft
führt' ich wohl Krieg:
doch Siegmund verfiel mir als Knecht!

(*Wotan makes another vehement gesture, and then is overcome by his sense of powerlessness.*)

For soul and body,
he is your servant,
and now must I
be subjected to him?
Am I his slave,
to smile when he scorns me?
despised by the world,

Der dir als Herren
hörig und eigen,
gehorchen soll ihm
dein ewig Gemahl?
Soll mich in Schmach
der Niedrigste schmähen,
dem Frechen zum Sporn,

and mocked by the free?	dem Freien zum Spott?
And can my husband allow me,	Das kann mein Gatte nicht wollen,
his goddess, to suffer this shame?	die Göttin entweiht er nicht so!

[36]

WOTAN
(gloomy)

What must I do?	Was verlangst du?

FRICKA

Abandon the Wälsung!	Lass von dem Wälsung!

[36]

WOTAN
(with muffled voice)

He goes his own way.	Er geh seines Wegs.

FRICKA

And you'll give him no help	Doch du schütze ihn nicht,
when he's called to defend his life?	wenn zur Schlacht ihn der Rächer ruft!

WOTAN

I'll give him no help.	Ich schütze ihn nicht.

FRICKA

Do not deceive me;	Sieh mir ins Auge,
look in my eyes;	sinne nicht Trug:
the Valkyrie leaves him to die!	die Walküre wend auch von ihm!

WOTAN

The Valkyrie is free to choose.	Das Walküre walte frei.

FRICKA

Not so; your commandment	Nicht doch; deinen Willen
is all she obeys:	vollbringt sie allein:
command her that Siegmund dies!	verbiete ihr Siegmunds Sieg!

WOTAN
(breaking out after a violent inner struggle)

I cannot destroy him;	Ich kann ihn nicht fällen:
he found my sword.	[27] er fand mein Schwert!

FRICKA

Destroy all its magic,	Entzieh dem den Zauber,
command it to break!	zerknick es dem Knecht!
Siegmund falls in the fight!	Schutzlos schau' ihn der Feind!

BRÜNNHILDE
(still invisible, calling from the heights) [34]

Hiaha! Hiaha! Hoyotoho!	[35] Heiaha! Heiaha! Hojotoho!

FRICKA

And here is your valiant maid,	Dort kommt deine kühne Maid;
joyfully coming this way.	jauchzend jagt sie daher.

BRÜNNHILDE

Hiaha! Hiaha!	Heiaha! Heiaha!
Hiohotoyo! Hotoyoha!	Heiohotojo! Hotojoha!

WOTAN
(dejected, to himself)

To fight now for Siegmund she rides.	Ich rief sie für Siegmund zu Ross!

(Brünnhilde appears, with her horse, on the rocky path to the right. On seeing Fricka, she breaks off suddenly and, during the following, she slowly, silently leads her horse down the mountain path, and then stables it in a cave.)

And her shield today	Deiner ew'gen Gattin
must shelter the honour	heilige Ehre
of your immortal wife!	beschirme heut ihr Schild!
For men in their scorn	Von Menschen verlacht,
would laugh at our might,	verlustig der Macht,
jeer at the glorious gods,	gingen wir Götter zugrund:
if today our warlike daughter	würde heut nicht hehr
should not revenge	und herrlich mein Recht
all the wrongs of your wife!	gerächt von der mutigen Maid.
The Wälsung dies for my honour!	[9] Der Wälsung fällt meiner Ehre!
Will Wotan now give me his oath?	Empfah ich von Wotan den Eid?

WOTAN

(throwing himself on a rocky seat in terrible dejection and inner agony) [36]

Take my oath!	Nimm den Eid!

(Fricka strides towards the back; there she meets Brünnhilde and stops for a moment before her.)

FRICKA
(to Brünnhilde)

Wotan is waiting there:	Heervater harret dein:
let him instruct you	lass ihn dir künden,
how the lot must be cast.	wie das Los er gekiest!

(She mounts her chariot and drives quickly away.) [23, 36]

Scene Two. *Brünnhilde advances with astonished and anxious mien to Wotan, who, leaning back on the rocky seat, his head propped on his hand, is sunk in gloomy brooding.*

BRÜNNHILDE

Fricka	Schlimm, fürcht ich,
has won the fight;	schloss der Streit,
since she smiles at the outcome.	[36] lachte Fricka dem Lose.
Father, what news	Vater, was soll
have you to tell me?	dein Kind erfahren?
Why this sadness and sorrow?	Trübe scheinst du und traurig!

WOTAN
(drops his arm helplessly and lets his head sink on his breast.)

I forged the fetters;	In eigner Fessel
now I'm bound.	fing ich mich,
I, least free of all living!	ich Unfreiester aller!

BRÜNNHILDE

What troubles you so;	So sah ich dich nie!
what new grief is this?	Was nagt dir das Herz?

WOTAN
(whose expression and gestures grow in intensity from this point, until they culminate in a fearful outburst.) [23]

Oh infinite shame!	O heilige Schmach!
Oh shameful distress!	O schmählicher Harm!
Gods' despair!	Götternot!
Gods' despair!	Götternot!
Endless remorse!	Endloser Grimm!
Grief evermore!	Ewiger Gram!
The saddest of beings is Wotan!	Der Traurigste bin ich von allen!

BRÜNNHILDE
(Terrified, she throws shield, spear and helmet from her and sinks at Wotan's feet in anxious solicitude.)

Father! Father!	Vater! Vater!
Tell me, what is it?	Sage, was ist dir?
For your daughter is filled with dismay!	Wie erschreckst du mit Sorge dein Kind?
Oh trust in me!	Vertraue mir!

You know I'm true!	Ich bin dir treu:
See, Brünnhilde begs you.	sieh, Brünnhilde bittet!

(She lays her head and hands with loving concern on his knees and lap.) [30a, b]

WOTAN
(looks long in her eyes, then strokes her hair with involuntary tenderness. As if coming to himself out of deep brooding, he begins softly:)

If I should tell you,	Lass ich's verlauten,
might I not lose	lös ich dann nicht
the controlling power of my will?	meines Willens haltenden Haft?

BRÜNNHILDE
(answers him equally softly)

To Wotan's will you're speaking;	Zu Wotans Willen sprichst du,
you can say what you will;	sagst du mir, was du willst;
what am I,	wer bin ich,
if not your will alone?	wär' ich dein Wille nicht?

WOTAN
(very softly)

These thoughts that I have never uttered,	Was deinem in Worten ich künde,
though I may think them,	unausgesprochen
still they're unspoken.	bleib es denn ewig:
I think aloud, then,	mit mir nur rat ich,
speaking to you. [36]	red ich zu dir.

(in a still more muted, fearful voice, while he gazes steadily into Brünnhilde's eyes)

When youth's delightful	Als junger Liebe
pleasures had waned,	Lust mir verblich,
I longed in my soul for might;	verlangte nach Macht mein Mut:
and driven	von jäher Wünsche
by impetuous desires,	Wüten gejagt,
I won myself the world;	gewann ich mir dir Welt.
yet all unwitting,	Unwissend trugvoll,
I acted wrongly;	Untreue übt' ich,
trusted in treaties	band durch Verträge,
where evil lay,	was Unheil barg:
craftily counselled by Loge,	listig verlockte mich Loge,
who lured me on—then left.	der schweifend nun verschwand.
Yet the longing [36]	Von der Liebe doch
for love would not leave me;	mocht' ich nicht lassen,
in my might I felt its enchantment.	in der Macht verlangt' ich nach Minne.
That child of night,	Den Nacht gebar,
the cringing Nibelung,	der bange Nibelung,
Alberich, broke from its bonds; [5]	Alberich, brach ihren Bund;
by cursing love	er fluchte der Liebe
he was able to gain	und gewann durch den Fluch
the Rhinemaids' glistering gold, [4]	des Rheines glänzendes Gold
and with that gold, all his power.	und mit ihm masslose Macht.
The ring that he made, [6]	Den Ring, den er schuf,
I cunningly stole it;	entriss ich ihm listig;
but to the Rhine	doch nicht dem Rhein
it was not returned.	gab ich ihn zurück:
I used the gold	mit ihm bezahlt' ich
to pay for Walhall, [8]	Walhalls Zinnen,
the hall the giants had built me,	der Burg, die Riesen mir bauten,
the hall where I rule all the world.	aus der ich der Welt nun gebot.
For one who knows [24]	Die alles weiss,
all things that were,	was einstens war,
Erda, the wisest,	Erda, die weihlich
holiest Wala,	weiseste Wala,
warned me away from the ring,	riet mir ab von dem Ring,
told of eternal disaster.	warnte vor ewigem Ende.
When I asked her to say more,	Von dem Ende wollt'ich
she vanished;	mehr noch wissen;
in silence she sank from my sight.	[36] doch schweigend entschwand mir das Weib.

Then I lost all my joy in life;
my only desire was to learn.
  So I made my way
  down into the depths;
  by love's enchantment
  I conquered the Wala,
humbled her silent pride,
till she told me all she knew.
Wisdom I won from her words;
the Wala demanded a pledge;
the wise Erda conceived
a daughter — Brünnhilde, you.
  With eight sisters
  you were brought up
  as bold Valkyries,
  who would avert
  the doom that Wala
  had made me fear —
the shameful defeat of the immortals.
  Our foes would find us
  ready for fight;
you would assemble my army:
  the men whom we held
  by our laws in bondage,
  the mortals, whom we
  had curbed in their pride,
  whom by treacherous treaties,
  shameful agreements,
  we'd bound in obedience
  blindly to serve us;
  and yours was the task
  to stir them to battle,
  and arouse brave men
  to ruthless war,
till valiant hosts of heroes
had gathered in Walhall's hall!

And that hall is guarded securely;
many a hero I brought.
  So why are you troubled,
  for we never failed?

There's more to tell;
mark what I say;
hear what the Wala foretold!
  For Alberich's host
  threatens our downfall;
  an envious rage
  burns in the Niblung.
  Yet I have no fear
  of his dusky battalions,
while my heroes keep me secure.
  But if once the ring
  returns to the Niblung,
he conquers Walhall for ever;
  by his curse on love,
  he alone
  can employ
  the ring's enchantment
  to bring eternal
  shame on the gods;
  my heroes' hearts
  he'd win for himself;
  he'd make my army

Da verlor ich den leichten Mut,
zu wissen begehrt' es den Gott:
  in den Schloss der Welt
  schwang ich mich hinab,
  mit Liebeszauber
  zwang ich die Wala,
stört' ihres Wissens Stolz,
dass sie Rede nun mir stand.
Kunde empfing ich von ihr;
von mir doch barg sie ein Pfand:
der Welt weisestes Weib
[30a] gebar mir, Brünnhilde, dich.
[34]   Mit acht Schwestern
  zog ich dich auf;
  durch euch Walküren
  wollt' ich wenden,
  was mir die Wala
  zu fürchten schuf:
ein schmähliches Ende der Ew'gen.
[34]   Dass stark zum Streit
  uns fände der Feind,
heiss ich euch Helden mir schaffen:
  die herrisch wir sonst
  in Gesetzen hielten,
  die Männer, denen
  den Mut wir gewehrt,
  die durch trüber Verträge
  trügende Bande
  zu blindem Gehorsam
  wir uns gebunden —
[34]   die solltet zu Sturm
  und Streit ihr nun stacheln,
  ihre Kraft reizen
  zu rauhem krieg,
dass kühner Kämpfer Scharen
[8] ich sammle in Walhalls Saal!

BRÜNNHILDE

Deinen Saal füllten wir weidlich:
viele schon führ' ich dir zu.
  Was macht dir nun Sorge,
  da nie wir gesäumt?

WOTAN

[24] Ein andres ist's:
  achte es wohl,
[6]   wes mich die Wala gewarnt!
  Durch Alberichs Heer
  droht uns das Ende:
  mit neidischem Grimm
  grollt mir der Niblung:
  doch scheu ich nun nicht
  seine nächtigen Scharen,
  meine Helden schüfen mir Sieg.
[6]   Nur wenn je den Ring
  zurück er gewänne,
  danne wäre Walhall verloren:
  Der der Liebe fluchte,
  er allein
  nützte neidisch
  des Ringes Runen
  zu aller Edlen
  endloser Schmach;
  der Helden Mut
  entwendet' er mir;
  die Kühnen selber

bend to his will,
and with that force
give battle to me.
So I pondered a way
to keep the ring from the Niblung.
  The giant Fafner,
one of the pair
for whose work I paid
the fatal gold —
Fafner broods on the gold
he murdered his brother to gain.
From him must the ring be taken,
that ring he won as his wages.
  Yet the bond that I made
forbids me to harm him;
if I should try
my power would fail.
These are the fetters
which have bound me;
since by my treaties I rule,
by those treaties I am enslaved.
  Yet one can accomplish
what I may not:
a man, a hero
I've never shie!ded,
whom I've not prompted,
foe to the gods,
free of soul,
fearless and bold,
who acts alone,
by his own design —
that man can do
what the god must shun;
though never urged by me,
he can achieve my desire!
  One at war with all gods,
he can save us!
This friendliest foe,
oh how can I find?
Oh where is this free one,
whom I've not shielded,
who in brave defiance
is dearest to me?
How can I create one,
who, not through me,
but on his own
can achieve my will?
Oh godly distress!
Sorrowful shame!
With loathing
I can find but myself
in all my hand has created!
This free one whom I have longed for,
this free one can never be found;
for I have no power to make him;
my hand can only make slaves!

[6] Sorgend sann ich nun selbst,
der Ring dem Feind zu entreissen.
[12]   Der Riesen einer,
denen ich einst
mit verfluchtem Gold
den Fleiss vergalt:
Fafner hütet den Hort,
um den er den Bruder gefällt.
Ihm müsst' ich den Reif entringen,
den selbst als Zoll ich ihm zahlte.
[15]   Doch mit dem ich vertrug,
ihn darf ich nicht treffen;
machtlos vor ihm
erläge mein Mut:
Das sind die Bande,
die mich binden:
[9] der durch Verträge ich Herr,
[36b, 27] den Verträgen bin ich nun Knecht.
  Nur einer könnte,
was ich nicht darf:
ein Held, dem helfend
nie ich mich neigte;
der fremd dem Gotte,
frei seiner Gunst,
unbewusst,
ohne Geheiss,
aus eigner Not,
mit der eignen Wehr
schüfe die Tat,
die ich scheuen muss,
die nie mein Rat ihm riet,
[36b] wünscht sie auch einzig mein Wunsch!
  Der, entgegen dem Gott,
für mich föchte,
den freundlichen Feind,
wie fände ich ihn?
Wie schüf' ich den Freien,
den nie ich schirmte,
der in eignem Trotze
der Trauteste mir?
Wie macht' ich den andren,
der nicht mehr ich,
und aus sich wirkte,
was ich nur will?
[5, 24] O göttliche Not!
Grässliche Schmach!
Zum Ekel find ich
ewig nur mich
in allem, was ich erwirke!
Das andre, das ich ersehne,
das andre erseh ich nie:
denn selbst muss der Freie sich schaffen;
[27x] Knechte erknet ich mir nur!

[24, 36]

BRÜNNHILDE

But the Wälsung, Siegmund,
  is he not free?

Doch der Wälsung, Siegmund,
[28] wirkt er nicht selbst?

WOTAN

Wild and free
was our life together;
I taught him to hate the gods,
urged his heart to rebel.

Wild durchschweift' ich
mit ihm die Wälder;
gegen der Götter Rat
reizte kühn ich ihn auf:

Now when the gods would kill him,   gegen der Götter Rache
all that he has is a sword;   [27a] schützt ihn nun einzig das Schwert,
(emphatic and bitter)

and yet that sword   das eines Gottes
was given by a god.   [36]   Gunst ihm beschied.
How could I hope   Wie wollt' ich listig
to win by deception?   selbst mich belügen?
The lie was revealed   So leicht ja entfrug mir
when Fricka appeared: Fricka den Trug:
I stood ashamed,   zu tiefster Scham
I had no reply!   durchschaute sie mich!
So to her I had to surrender.   Ihrem Willen muss ich gewähren.

BRÜNNHILDE

Then Siegmund must fall in his fight?   So nimmst du von Siegmund den Sieg?

WOTAN

I set hands on Alberich's ring,   [6]   Ich berührte Alberichs Ring,
grasped in greed at the gold.   gierig hielt ich das Gold!
The curse that I fled   [30a]   Der Fluch, den ich floh,
has fastened on me.   nicht flieht er nun mich:
Though I love him, I must forsake him;   Was ich liebe, muss ich verlassen,
murder the son I love so;   morden, wen je ich minne,
basely betray him   trügend verraten
when he trusts!   [23]   wer mir traut!
(Wotan's demeanour changes from the expression of the most terrible suffering to that of despair.) [27]

Fade from my sight,   Fahre denn hin,
honour and fame,   herrische Pracht,
glorious godhead's   göttlichen Prunkes
glittering shame!   prahlende Schmach!
And fall in ruins,   Zusammenbreche,
all I have raised!   was ich gebaut!
I leave all my work;   Auf geb ich mein Werk;
but one thing I desire: nur eines will ich noch:
the ending,   [27b]   das Ende,
that ending!   das Ende!
(He pauses in thought.) [24]

And to that ending   Und für das Ende
works Alberich!   sorgt Alberich!
Now I grasp   Jetzt versteh ich
all the secret sense   den stummen Sinn
that filled the words of the Wala: [22] des wilden Wortes der Wala:
'When the dusky foe of love   'Wenn der Liebe finstrer Feind
gains in hatred a son,   zürnend zeugt einen Sohn,
the gods may know   der Sel'gen Ende
their doom is near.'   [27a, 32, 8, 3] säumt dann nicht!'
From Nibelheim   Vom Niblung jüngst
the tidings have come   vernahm ich die Mär,
that the dwarf has forced a woman;   dass ein Weib der Zwerg bewältigt,
his gold bought her embrace;   des Gunst Gold ihm erzwang:
and she will bear   [22]   des Hasses Frucht
Alberich's son;   hegt eine Frau,
the seed of spite   des Neides Kraft
stirs in her womb;   kreisst ihr im Schloss:
this wonder befell   das Wunder gelang
the loveless Niblung;   dem Liebelosen;
while I, who loved so truly,   doch der in Lieb' ich freite,
my free son I never could win.   den Freien erlang ich mir nicht.
(rising up in bitter wrath)

I give you my blessing,   [32, 8, 3] So nimm meinen Segen,
Nibelung son!   Niblungen-Sohn!
Let all that irks me   Was tief mich ekelt,
be yours to inherit;   dir geb ich's zum Erbe,
in Walhall's glorious halls   der Gottheit nichtigen Glanz:
achieve your unhallowed desires!   zernage ihn gierig dein Neid!

80

Oh speak, father,
and tell me my task.

O sag, künde,
was soll nun dein Kind?

WOTAN
(*bitterly*)

Fight boldly for Fricka,
guardian of wedlock's vow!

Fromm streite für Fricka;
hüte ihr Eh' und Eid!

(*drily*)

The choice she made,
that choice must be mine:
my own desires are but useless.
Since that free one I cannot fashion,
be Fricka's champion,
fight for her slave!

Was sie erkor,
das kiese auch ich:
was frommte mir eigner Wille?
Einen Freien kann ich nicht wollen:
für Frickas Knechte
kämpfe nun du!

BRÜNNHILDE

No, have mercy,
take back your word!
You love Siegmund;
let your love
command me: fight for the Wälsung.

Weh! Nimm reuig
zurück das Wort!
Du liebst Siegmund;
dir zulieb,
ich weiss es, schütz ich den Wälsung.

WOTAN

You must conquer Siegmund,
and Hunding must win in the fight!
Guard yourself well,
be stern and strong;
bring all your boldness
and force to the fight:
a strong sword
has Siegmund;
he'll not easily yield!

Fällen sollst du Siegmund,
für Hunding erfechten den Sieg!
Hüte dich wohl
und halte dich stark,
all deiner Kühnheit
entbiete im Kampf:
[27] ein Siegschwert
schwingt Siegmund;
schwerlich fällt er dir feig!

BRÜNNHILDE

Him you have always
taught me to love;
for his noble courage
and valour you love him;
if you ask me to kill him,
then I shall refuse!

Den du zu lieben
stets mich gelehrt,
der in hehrer Tugend
dem Herzen dir teuer —
gegen ihn zwingt mich nimmer
dein zwiespältig Wort!

WOTAN

Rebellious child!
Do as I say!
What are you but the obedient,
blind slave of my will?
When I told my sorrows,
sank I so low,
that I'm scorned, defied
by the child whom I raised?
Daughter, know you my wrath?
Your soul would be crushed
if you confronted
that fierce, furious rage!
Within my bosom
anger is hid,
that could lay to waste
all of a world —
that world I once used to love:
woe to him whom it strikes!
He would pay for his pride!
I warn you, then,
rouse not my rage!

Ha, Freche du!
Frevelst du mir?
Wer bist du, als meines Willens
[9] blind wählende Kür?
Da mit dir ich tagte,
sank ich so tief,
dass zum Schimpf der eignen
Geschöpfe ich ward?
Kennst du, Kind, meinen Zorn?
Verzage dein Mut,
wenn je zermalmend
auf dich stürzte sein Strahl!
In meinem Busen
berg ich den Grimm,
der in Grau'n und Wust
wirft eine Welt,
die einst zur Lust mir gelacht:
Wehe dem, den er trifft!
[36b] Trauer schüf' ihm sein Trotz!
Drum rat ich dir,
reize mich nicht!

But swiftly do my command.	Besorge, was ich befahl:
Siegmund's fated!	[27x] Siegmund falle!
That is the Valkyrie's work!	Dies sei der Walküre Werk!

(He storms away, and quickly disappears among the crags to the left.)
[36b, 8, 35, 36]

BRÜNNHILDE
(stands for a long time, shocked and stunned.)

So I obey his command;	So sah ich Siegvater nie,
such rage I've never seen before.	[36, 34] erzürnt' ihn sonst wohl auch ein Zank!

(She stoops down sadly, and takes up her weapons, with which she arms herself again.)

Shield, spear	Schwer wiegt mir
seem to weigh me down!	der Waffen Wucht.
In a joyful fight	Wenn nach Lust ich focht,
I found they were light!	wie waren sie leicht!
This hateful task	Zu böser Schlacht
fills my heart with fear.	schleich ich heut so bang.

(She gazes thoughtfully before her, and sighs.) [31]

Woe, my Wälsung!	[36] Weh, mein Wälsung!
In deepest sorrow	Im höchsten Leid
this true one must falsely betray you!	muss dich treulos die Treue verlassen!

(She turns slowly towards the back.) [36b]

Scene Three. *Arrived at the rocky pass, Brünnhilde, looking into the gorge, perceives Siegmund and Sieglinde; she watches their approach for a moment and then goes into the cave to her horse, disappearing from the audience. Siegmund and Sieglinde appear on the pass. Sieglinde comes hastily forward; Siegmund tries to restrain her.* [11b, 30a]

SIEGMUND

Rest for a while;	Raste nur hier;
stay by my side!	gönne dir Ruh!

SIEGLINDE

Further! Further!	Weiter! Weiter!

SIEGMUND
(He embraces her with gentle force.)

No further now!	Nicht weiter nun!

(He clasps her firmly to him.)

Oh trust me, sweet, loving bride!	Verweile, süssestes Weib!
In bliss I embraced you,	Aus Wonne-Entzücken
then you escaped;	zucktest du auf,
with frenzied haste	mit jäher Hast
fled from my arms,	jagtest du fort:
so fast I could scarce pursue;	kaum folgt' ich der wilden Flucht;
through wood and field,	durch Wald und Flur,
over rock and stone,	über Fels und Stein,
speechless, silent,	sprachlos, schweigend
flying ahead;	sprangst du dahin,
I called you all in vain!	kein Ruf hielt dich zur Rast!
Now you must rest:	Ruhe nun aus:
speak but a word,	rede zu mir!
ending this silent dread!	[30] Ende des Schweigens Angst!
See, your brother	Sieh, dein Bruder
shelters his bride:	hält seine Braut:
Siegmund guards you from harm!	Siegmund ist dir Gesell!

(Without her noticing, he has drawn her to the rocky seat.)

SIEGLINDE
(She gazes with growing rapture into Siegmund's eyes, then throws her arms passionately round his neck and so remains. Then she starts up in sudden terror.)

Away! Away!	Hinweg! Hinweg!
Fly from the cursed one!	Flieh die Entweihte!

Unholy
this form that you clasp;
disgraced, dishonoured,
dead in my heart.
Cast me from you,
fling me aside!
Let winds waft me away,
for I have defiled your embrace!
When in your loving embrace
such blissful delight I found,
you gave me all of your heart,
and all my love was awaked.
In that holy enchantment,
sweetest rapture,
when all my soul
and senses were won,
loathing and horror
for shameful dishonour
struck with dismay
this traitorous woman,
whom Hunding owned as a wife,
who loveless lay in his arms!
Fly from the cursed one,
far let her flee!
Dishonoured am I,
bereft of grace:
the purest hero
I must abandon,
for how can this guilty wife
dare to love him?
Shame I'd bring to my brother,
shame to him whom I love!

Unheilig!
umfängt dich ihr Arm;
entehrt, geschändet
schwand dieser Leib:
flieh die Leiche,
lasse sie los!
Der Wind mag sie verwehn,
[30a] die ehrlos dem Edlen sich gab!
Da er sie liebend umfing,
da seligste Lust sie fand,
da ganz sie minnte der Mann,
der ganz ihre Minne geweckte:
vor der süssesten Wonne
heiligster Weihe,
die ganz ihr Sinn
und Seele durchdrang,
Grauen und Schauder
ob grässlichster Schande
musste mit Schreck
die Schmähliche fassen,
die je dem Manne gehorcht,
der ohne Minne sie hielt!
Lass die Verfluchte,
lass sie dich fliehn!
Verworfen bin ich,
der Würde bar!
Dir reinstem Manne
muss ich entrinnen,
dir Herrlichem darf ich
nimmer gehören.
Schande bring ich dem Bruder,
Schmach dem freienden Freund!

[33]

SIEGMUND

But this shame you have felt,
this shame shall be paid by blood!
So flee you no further;
Hunding shall find us;
here I shall defeat him:
with Notung
I shall pierce his heart;
vengeance then you will have won!

Was je Schande dir schuf,
das büsst nun des Frevlers Blut!
Drum fliehe nicht weiter;
harre des Feindes;
hier soll er mir fallen:
Wenn Notung ihm
[27] das Herz zernagt,
Rache dann hast du erreicht!

SIEGLINDE
(*She starts up and listens.*) [32]

Hark! The horn call!
Do you not hear?
All around,
cries of revenge,
from wood and dale,
ring in my ears.
Hunding has wakened
from heavy sleep!
Hunters, I hear them;
all have assembled:
hard on the trail,
dogs are howling;
they lead the avengers;
they will kill us for breaking a vow!

Horch, die Hörner!
Hörst du den Ruf?
Ringsher tönt
wütend Getös';
aus Wald und Gau
gellt es herauf.
Hunding erwachte
aus hartem Schlaf!
Sippen und Hunde
ruft er zusammen;
mutig gehetzt
heult die Meute,
wild bellt sie zum Himmel
um der Ehe gebrochenen Eid!

(*As if crazed, she stares before her.*)

Where are you, Siegmund?
Are you still here?
bravest of lovers,
true, tender brother!
With your glorious eyes

Wo bist du, Siegmund?
Seh ich dich noch,
brünstig geliebter,
leuchtender Bruder?
Deines Auges Stern

83

for the last time behold me:
  do not refuse
this accursed woman's kiss!
	lass noch einmal mir strahlen:
	  wehre dem Kuss
	des verworfnen Weibes nicht!

(*She throws herself sobbing on his breast, then starts up again in terror.*)

Hear! Again		Horch, o horch!
That is Hunding's horn!		Das ist Hundings Horn!
And the huntsmen	[36]	Seine Meute naht
come to take your life;		mit mächt'ger Wehr:
no sword helps you		Kein Schwert frommt
against the hounds;		vor der Hunde Schwall:
let it go, Siegmund!		wirf es fort, Siegmund!
Siegmund, where are you?	[24]	Siegmund, wo bist du?
Ah there! I see you now!		Ha dort! Ich sehe dich!
Fearful the sight!		Schrecklich Gesicht!
Dogs have fastened		Rüden fletschen
their teeth in your flesh;		die Zähne nach Fleisch;
they take no heed		sie achten nicht
of your noble glance;		deines edlen Blicks;
all around you leaping		bei den Füssen packt dich
to tear at your throat —		das feste Gebiss —
you fall —		du fällst —
in splinters the shining sword!		in Stücken zerstaucht das Schwert. —
The ash is down —	[27]	Die Esche stürzt —
the tree destroyed! —		es bricht der Stamm! —
Brother! My brother!		Bruder, mein Bruder!
Siegmund — ah! —		Siegmund — ha! —

(*She sinks senseless into Siegmund's arms.*)

SIEGMUND

Sister! Beloved!	[30a]	Schwester! Geliebte!

(*He listens to her breathing and makes sure that she is still alive. He lets her slide downwards so that, as he himself sinks into a sitting posture, her head rests on his lap. In this position they both remain until the end of the following scene. A long silence, during which Siegmund bends over Sieglinde with tender care, and presses a long kiss on her brow.*) [38, 37]

Scene Four. *Brünnhilde, leading her horse by the bridle, comes out of the cave and advances slowly and solemnly forwards. She pauses and observes Siegmund from a distance. She again slowly advances. She stops, somewhat nearer. She carries her shield and spear in one hand, resting the other on her horse's neck, and thus she gravely regards Siegmund.* [8]

BRÜNNHILDE

Siegmund!		Siegmund,
Look on me!	[38]	sieh auf mich!
I come		Ich bin's
to call you hence.		der bald du folgst.

SIEGMUND
(*He raises his eyes to her.*)

Who are you, say,	[37]	Wer bist du, sag,
who so stern and beauteous appear?		die so schön und ernst mir erscheint?

BRÜNNHILDE

Those doomed to death		Nur Todgeweihten
alone can see me;		taugt mein Anblick;
who meets my gaze		wer mich erschaut,
must turn from the light of life.		der scheidet vom Lebenslicht.
I appear in the fight	[8]	Auf der Walstatt allein
to death-doomed heroes:		erschein ich Edlen:
those whom I choose		wer mich gewahrt,
have no choice but to die!		zur Wal kor ich ihn mir!

SIEGMUND
(*looks long, firmly, and searchingly into her eyes, then bows his head in thought, and at length turns resolutely to her again.*) [38]

And if I come,	[37]	Der dir nun folgt,
tell me, where will you lead me?		wohin führst du den Helden?

To Wotan,
who marks you for his.
He commands:
to Walhall come with me.

[8] Zu Walvater,
der dich gewählt,
führ ich dich:
nach Walhall folgst du mir.

SIEGMUND

To Walhall's hall?
Does Wotan rule there alone?

In Walhalls Saal
Walvater find ich allein?

BRÜNNHILDE

The fallen heroes
dwell there too;
they'll welcome you
and greet you to their band.

Gefallner Helden
hehre Schar
umfängt dich hold
mit hochheiligem Gruss.

[34]

SIEGMUND

And shall I find there
Wälse, my noble father?

Fänd' ich in Walhall
Wälse, den eignen Vater?

BRÜNNHILDE

Your father waits there
to greet his son!

[8] Den Vater findet
der Wälsung dort.

SIEGMUND

Are there in Walhall,
maidens as well?

Grüss mich in Walhall
froh eine Frau?

BRÜNNHILDE

Fair maidens
wait on you there.
Wotan's daughter,
she will bring you the cup!

[11a] Wunschmädchen
walten dort hehr:
Wotans Tochter
reicht dir traulich den Trank!

SIEGMUND

Fair goddess
with awe I salute you
as Wotan's child;
but one thing tell me, immortal!
This brother is blessed
by his bride and his sister.
You call Siegmund —
Sieglinde too?

Hehr bist du,
und heilig gewahr ich
das Wotanskind:
doch eines sag mir, du Ew'ge!
[37] Begleitet den Bruder
die bräutliche Schwester?
Umfängt Siegmund
Sieglinde dort?

BRÜNNHILDE

Here on earth
you have to leave her:
Sieglinde sees
Siegmund no more.

Erdenluft
muss sie noch atmen:
[38] Sieglinde sieht
Siegmund dort nicht!

[30b]

SIEGMUND
(*He bends softly over Sieglinde, kisses her gently on the brow, and again turns calmly to Brünnhilde.*)

Then greet for me Walhall,
greet for me Wotan,
greet for me Wälse
and all the heroes;
greet all those fair
and lovely maidens.
To Walhall I will not go!

[8] So grüsse mir Walhall,
grüsse mir Wotan,
grüsse mir Wälse
und alle Helden,
grüsse auch die holden
[11a] Wunschesmädchen:
[38] zu ihnen folg ich dir nicht.

BRÜNNHILDE

You gazed on the Valkyrie's

[37] Du sahest der Walküre

85

searing glance,	sehrenden Blick:
and now you have no choice.	mit ihr musst du nun ziehn!

SIEGMUND

Where Sieglinde lives	[30]	Wo Sieglinde lebt
in joy or pain:		in Lust und Leid,
there must Siegmund live with her:		da will Siegmund auch säumen.
I've gazed on your glance;	[38]	Noch machte dein Blick
I do not fear you:		nicht mich erbleichen:
you cannot force me to go!		vom Bleiben zwingt er mich nie!

BRÜNNHILDE

I cannot force,		Solang du lebst,
not while you live;		zwäng' dich wohl nichts:
but death can force you to go!	[37]	doch zwingt dich Toren der Tod:
I come to warn you		ihn dir zu künden,
death is near.		kam ich her.

SIEGMUND

And who is the man	Wo wäre der Held,
who'll take my life?	dem heut ich fiel'?

BRÜNNHILDE

Hunding kills you today.	[38]	Hunding fällt dich im Streit.

SIEGMUND

Do you think I'm threatened	Mit stärkrem drohe
by Hunding's anger?	als Hundings Streichen!
If you lurk here,	Lauerst du hier
lusting for blood,	lüstern auf Wal,
choose that man as your prey:	jenen kiese zum Fang:
I know he will fall in the fight!	ich denk ihn zu fällen im Kampf!

BRÜNNHILDE
(*shaking her head*)

You, Wälsung,	Dir, Wälsung,
hear what I say:	höre mich wohl:
you have been marked for death.	dir ward das Los gekiest.

SIEGMUND

I have a sword!	[27]	Kennst du dies Schwert?
My father's gift		Der mir es schuf,
will guard me well:		beschied mir Sieg:
I defy your threats with the sword!		deinem Drohen trotz ich mit ihm!

BRÜNNHILDE
(*with solemn emphasis*)

Gift of the god	Der dir es schuf,
who ordered your death;	beschied dir jetzt Tod:
and he takes his spell from the sword!	seine Tugend nimmt er dem Schwert!

SIEGMUND
(*vehemently*)

Still! You'll waken		Schweig und schrecke
my sister from sleep!	[30a]	die Schlummernde nicht!

(*He bends tenderly, in an outburst of grief, over Sieglinde.*)

Woe! Woe!	Weh! Weh!
Sister and bride,	Süssestes Weib,
you saddest of all trusting women!	du traurigste aller Getreuen!
Though the world rises	Gegen dich wütet
against you in arms,	in Waffen die Welt:
yet I, whom alone you could trust,	und ich, dem du einzig vertraut,
yes, I, who have brought you this pain,	für den du ihr einzig getrozt,
am not allowed	mit meinem Schutz
to shield you from danger,	nicht soll ich dich schirmen,
but told I must fall in the fight!	die Kühne verraten im Kampf?

Then shame on him	Ha, Schande ihm,
who bestowed the sword,	der das Schwert mir schuf,
the sword that will bring my shame!	beschied er mir Schimpf für Sieg!
Yet though I die here,	Muss ich denn fallen,
I'll not go to Walhall:	nicht fahr ich nach Walhall:
hell may hold me instead!	Hella halte mich fest!

(He bends low over Sieglinde.) [30a/11b]

BRÜNNHILDE
(shocked) [38]

So you would sacrifice	So wenig achtest du
joy everlasting?	ewige Wonne?

(slowly and hesitatingly)

Is she all	Alles wär' dir
in the world to you,	das arme Weib,
that maid who lies there	das müd und harmvoll
limp and afraid in your arms?	matt von dem Schosse dir hängt?
You'd leave Walhall for her?	Nichts sonst hieltest du hehr?

SIEGMUND
(looking up at her bitterly) [11]

So young and fair [37]	So jung und schön
you seem to my eyes;	erschimmerst du mir:
but how cold and hard	doch wie kalt und hart
I know in my heart!	erkennt dich mein Herz.
You came to mock me;	Kannst du nur höhnen,
now leave me alone,	so hebe dich fort,
you heartless, cold, cruel maid!	du arge, fühllose Maid!
But if it delights you	Doch musst du dich weiden
to watch my woe,	an meinem Weh,
you're free to feed on my pain;	mein Leiden letze dich denn;
may my grief gladden	meine Not labe
your envious heart;	dein neidvolles Herz:
but of Walhall's loveless pleasures	nur von Walhalls spröden Wonnen
you need tell me no more!	sprich du wahrlich mir nicht!

BRÜNNHILDE

I see the distress [30a/11]	Ich sehe die Not,
and grief in your heart,	die das Herz dir zernagt,
I feel all your suffering,	ich fühle des Helden
share in your pain!	heiligen Harm —
Siegmund, I'll care for your wife;	Siegmund, befiehl mir dein Weib;
I'll shield her safely from harm.	mein Schutz umfange sie fest!

SIEGMUND

So long as she lives	Kein andrer als ich
I'll allow no other to touch her:	soll die Reine lebend berühren:
if I have to die,	Verfiel ich dem Tod,
I will kill her first while she sleeps.	die Betäubte töt ich zuvor!

BRÜNNHILDE
(with increasing emotion)

Wälsung! Madman!	Wälsung! Rasender!
Hear my advice:	Hör meinen Rat:
I'll care for your wife;	befiehl mir dein Weib
I will shield her safely;	um des Pfandes willen,
a son shall be born from your love. [25]	das wonnig von dir es empfing.

SIEGMUND
(drawing his sword)

This sword, [27]	Dies Schwert,
which a traitor bestowed on the true;	das dem Treuen ein Trigvoller schuf;
this sword	dies Schwert,
that fails me when faced with a fight:	das feig vor dem Feind mich verrät:
since it must fail on my foe,	frommt es nich gegen den Feind,
I'll use it instead on a friend!	[27] so fromm es denn wider den Freund!

(He aims the sword at Sieglinde.)

Two lives	Zwei Leben
now lie in your power;	lachen dir hier:
take them, Notung,	nimm sie, Notung,
glittering blade!	neidischer Stahl!
Two with a single stroke!	Nimm sie mit einem Streich!

BRÜNNHILDE
(in a passionate outburst of sympathy)

Oh stay, Wälsung!	[38]	Halt ein, Wälsung!
Hear what I say!		Höre mein Wort!
Sieglinde lives then —		Sieglinde lebe —
and Siegmund lives by her side!		und Siegmund lebe mit ihr!
The choice is mine;		Beschlossen ist's;
and fate is altered;		das Schlachtlos wend ich:
you, Siegmund,		dir, Siegmund,
take my blessing, and win!		schaff ich Segen und Sieg!

(Horn-calls resound in the far distance.)

Hark to the call!	Hörst du den Ruf?
Prepare for your fight!	Nun rüste dich, Held!
Trust in the sword	Traue dem Schwert
and strike at his heart.	und schwing es getrost:
Your sword shall be true,	treu hält dir die Wehr,
and the Valkyrie is true as well!	wie die Walküre treu dich schützt!
Farewell, Siegmund,	Leb wohl, Siegmund,
hero I love!	seligster Held!
I will meet you there in the battle!	Auf der Walstatt seh ich dich wieder!

(She rushes away, and disappears with her horse into a ravine on the right. Siegmund looks after her with joy and exaltation. The stage has gradually darkened; heavy stormclouds sink down in the background, gradually veiling the cliffs, ravine, and rocky pass completely from view.) [30, 38]

Scene Five.

SIEGMUND
(bending over Sieglinde, listening to her breathing)

Charms of sleep		Zauberfest
are sent to soothe		bezähmt ein Schlaf
my sister's grief and pain.		der Holden Schmerz und Harm.
Did the Valkyrie cast this spell	[30b]	Da die Walküre zu mir trat,
and lull my beloved to sleep,		schuf sie ihr den wonnigen Trost?
so that no sound of our fight	[38]	Sollte die grimmige Wal
should frighten this suffering maid?		nicht schrecken ein gramvolles Weib?
Lifeless seems she,		Leblos scheint sie,
though still alive;		die dennoch lebt:
her sorrow is eased;		der Traurigen kost
she smiles in her sleep.		ein lächelnder Traum.
So peacefully sleep		So schlummre nun fort,
till the fight is fought;		bis die Schlacht gekämpft
then wake when I have won!	[11]	und Friede dich erfreu'!

(He lays her gently on the rocky seat and kisses her forehead in farewell. He hears Hunding's horn-call, and starts up resolutely.) [32]

I hear your call;	Der dort mich ruft,
guard yourself well;	rüste sich nun;
all you deserve	was ihm gebührt,
comes to you.	biet ich ihm:
Notung pays all my debt!	Notung zahl' ihm den Zoll!

(He draws his sword, [7, 32] hastens to the background, and, on reaching the pass, disappears in the dark stormcloud, from which a flash of lightning immediately breaks.)

SIEGLINDE
(begins to move restlessly in her dreams.)

Why doesn't father return?		Kehrte der Vater nur heim!
With the boy he is still in the woods.	[32]	Mit dem Knaben noch weilt er im Forst.
Mother! Mother!		Mutter, Mutter!
I feel afraid;		Mir bangt der Mut:

they seem unfriendly —	[30b]	Nicht freund und friedlich
who are the strangers?		scheimen die Fremden!
Smoky darkness —		Schwarze Dämpfe —
smouldering fires —		schwüles Gedünst —
now they are flaring,		feurige Lohe
flaming around —		leckt schon nach uns —
they burn the house —		es brennt das Haus —
Oh help me, brother!		zu Hilfe, Bruder!
Siegmund! Siegmund!		Siegmund! Siegmund!

(She leaps up. Violent thunder and lightning.)

Siegmund! Ah!   Siegmund! Ha!

(She stares about her in terror; nearly the whole stage is covered with black thunderclouds, the lightning and thunder continue. Hunding's horn-call sounds near.)

HUNDING'S VOICE
(in the background, from the pass)

Wehwalt! Wehwalt!	[5]	Wehwalt! Wehwalt!
Stand there and fight,		Steh mir zum Streit,
else with my hounds I will hunt you.		sollen dich Hunde nicht halten!

SIEGMUND'S VOICE
(from further off in the ravine)

Then show yourself;	Wo birgst du dich,
I've come in search of you!	dass ich vorbei dir schoss?
Stand and let me face you!	Steh, dass ich dich stelle!

SIEGLINDE
(listening in fearful agitation)

Hunding! Siegmund!	Hunding! Siegmund!
Could I but see them!	Könnt' ich sie sehen!

HUNDING

Come here, you treacherous lover!	Hierher, du frevelnder Freier!
Fricka claims you as prize.	Fricka fälle dich hier!

SIEGMUND
(now likewise from the pass)

Do you think that I'm weaponless,		Noch wähnst du mich waffenlos,
boasting fool?		feiger Wicht?
Don't call on Fricka,		Drohst du mit Frauen,
but fight your own fight;		so ficht nun selber,
no help from Fricka today!		sonst lässt dich Fricka im Stich!
For see, in your house		Denn sieh: deines Hauses
I drew from the tree	[27]	heimischem Stamm
the strongest, sharpest of swords,		entzog ich zaglos das Schwert;
and its sharpness strikes at your life!		seine Schneide schmecke jetzt du!

(A flash of lightning illumines the pass for a moment, and Hunding and Siegmund are seen fighting there.)

SIEGLINDE
(with her utmost force)

Stop the fight, you madmen!	Haltet ein, ihr Männer!
Murder me first!	Mordet erst mich!

(She rushes towards the pass, but suddenly, from above the combatants, on the right, a flash breaks forth so vividly that she staggers aside as if blinded. In the blaze of light Brünnhilde appears, hovering over Siegmund and protecting him with her shield.)

BRÜNNHILDE

Strike him, Siegmund!	Triff ihn, Siegmund!
Trust in the sword!	Traue dem Schwert!

(Just as Siegmund aims a deadly blow at Hunding, a glowing red light breaks from the left through the clouds, in which Wotan appears, standing over Hunding, holding his spear diagonally out at Siegmund.) [34, 27]

WOTAN

Away from the spear!	Zurück vor dem Speer!
I shatter the sword!	In Stücken das Schwert!

(*Brünnhilde, with her spear, recoils in terror before Wotan. Siegmund's sword shatters on the outstretched spear. Hunding plunges his spear into the unarmed man's breast. Siegmund falls dead to the ground. Sieglinde, who has heard his death-sigh, falls with a cry, as if lifeless, to the ground. As Siegmund falls, the glowing lights on either side disappear at once; a cloud of thick darkness rolls forward; in it, Brünnhilde is indistinctly seen, as she turns in haste to Sieglinde.*)

[9, 27, 5, 33, 38]

BRÜNNHILDE

To horse! Come, let me save you!	Zu Ross, dass ich dich rette!

(*She lifts Sieglinde quickly on to her horse, which is standing near the side gorge, and immediately disappears with her. At this moment the clouds part in the middle, so that Hunding, who had just drawn his spear from the fallen Siegmund's breast, is clearly seen. Wotan, surrounded by clouds, stands on a rock behind him, leaning on his spear and gazing sorrowfully at Siegmund's corpse.*) [24, 34, 38]

WOTAN
(*to Hunding*)

Go hence, slave!	Geh hin, Knecht!
Kneel before Fricka:	Knie vor Fricka:
tell her that Wotan's spear	meld ihr, dass Wotans Speer
avenged her cause of shame.	[9] gerächt, was Spott ihr schuf.
Go! Go!	Geh! Geh!

(*At the contemptuous wave of his wand, Hunding falls dead to the ground. Wotan, suddenly breaking out in terrible rage:*) [36]

But Brünnhilde!	Doch Brünnhilde!
Where is the guilty one?	Weh der Verbrecherin!
Fearful is the fate	Furchtbar sei
I'll pronounce	die Freche gestraft,
when she is caught in her flight!	[9] erreicht mein Ross ihre Flucht!

[36b]

(*He disappears in thunder and lightning. The curtain falls rapidly.*)

Act Two in the production at Covent Garden by Götz Friedrich, designed by Josef Svoboda with costumes designed by Ingrid Rosell (photo: Donald Southern)

Act Three

On the summit of a rocky mountain. On the right, a pinewood bounds the stage. On the left, the entrance to a cave which looks like a natural room; above it, the rock rises to its highest point. At the back the view is entirely open; rocks of various heights border a precipice, which, it is to be assumed, falls steeply to the background. Occasional cloudbanks fly past the mountain peak, as if driven by storm. Gerhilde, Ortlinde, Waltraute, and Schwertleite have assembled on the peak, by and above the cave: they are in full armour. **Scene One.** [34]

GERHILDE
(on the highest point, calling towards the background, where a thick cloud is passing)

Hoyotoho! Hoyotoho!	[35, 34]	Hojotoho! Hojotoho!
Hiaha! Hiaha!		Heiaha! Heiaha!
Helmwige! Here!		Helmwige! Hier!
Come here with your horse!		Hierher mit dem Ross!

HELMWIGE'S VOICE
(in the background)

Hoyotoho! Hoyotoho!	Hojotoho! Hojotoho!
Hiaha!	Heiaha!

(A flash of lightning breaks through the cloud; in its light, a Valkyrie on horseback becomes visible; on her saddle hangs a slain warrior. The apparition comes closer, moving from left to right past the rocky ridge.)

GERHILDE, WALTRAUTE, SCHWERTLEITE
(calling to the newcomer)

Hiaha! Hiaha!	Heiaha! Heiaha!

(The cloud with the apparition has disappeared to the right, behind the wood.)

ORTLINDE
(calling into the wood)

Go tether your chestnut	Zu Ortlindes Stute
next to my grey;	stell deinen Hengst:
she will be glad	mit meiner Grauen
to graze by your stallion.	grast gern dein Brauner!

WALTRAUTE
(calling into the wood)

Who hangs from your saddle?	Wer hängt dir im Sattel?

HELMWIGE
(coming from the wood)

Sintolt the Hegeling!	Sintolt, der Hegeling!

SCHWERTLEITE

Far from the grey	Führ deinen Brauen
then fasten your stallion;	fort von der Grauen:
Ortlinde's mare	Ortlindes Mähre
carries Wittig the Irming!	trägt Wittig, den Irming!

GERHILDE
(has come down lower.)

Implacable foes	Als Feinde nur sah ich
were Sintolt and Wittig!	Sintolt und Wittig!

ORTLINDE
(leaps up.)

Hiaha! Your stallion	[34]	Heiaha! Die Stute
is biting my mare!		stösst mir der Hengst!

(She runs into the wood. Gerhilde, Helmwige, and Schwertleite break into laughter.)
[35]

GERHILDE

The warriors' war	Der Recken Zwist
has spread to the horses!	entzweit noch die Rosse!

HELMWIGE
(calling back into the wood)

Quiet, Bruno!	Ruhig, Brauner!
Battle is over.	Brich nicht den Frieden.

WALTRAUTE
(On the highest point, where she has taken over from Gerhilde as watcher, she calls to the right side of the background.)

Hoyoho! Hoyoho!		Hojoho! Hojoho!
Siegrune, here!		Siegrune, hier!
What kept you so long?	[34]	Wo säumst du so lang?

(She listens to the right.)

SIEGRUNE'S VOICE
(from the right side of the background)

Work to do!	Arbeit gab's!
Have the others arrived?	Sind die andren schon da?

SCHWERTLEITE, WALTRAUTE
(calling to the right of the background)

Hoyotoho! Hoyotoho!	[35]	Hojotoho! Hojotoho!
Hiaha!		Heiaha!

GERHILDE

Hiaha!	Heiaha!

(Their gestures, as well as a bright glow behind the wood, show that Siegrune has just arrived there. From the distance below, two voices are heard at once.)

GRIMGERDE, ROSSWEISSE
(left, in the background)

Hoyotoho! Hoyotoho!	[35, 34]	Hojotoho! Hojotoho!
Hiaha!		Heiaha!

WALTRAUTE

Grimgerd and Rossweisse!	Grimgerd und Rossweisse!

GERHILDE

They're riding abreast.	Sie reiten zu zwei.

(In a cloudbank lit by lightning, moving past from the left, Grimgerde and Rossweisse appear, similarly on horseback, each with a dead warrior on her saddle. Helmwige, Ortlinde, and Siegrune come from the wood and greet the newcomers from the rocky ridge.)

HELMWIGE, ORTLINDE, SIEGRUNE

We greet the travellers!	Gegrüsst, ihr Reisige!
Rossweisse and Grimgerde!	Rossweiss und Grimgerde!

ROSSWEISSE'S AND GRIMGERDE'S VOICES

Hoyotoho! Hoyotoho!	Hojotoho! Hojotoho!
Hiaha!	Heiaha!

(The apparition disappears behind the wood.)

THE OTHER SIX VALKYRIES

Hoyotoho! Hoyotoho!	Hojotoho! Hojotoho!
Hiaha!	Heiaha!

GERHILDE
(calling into the wood)

Now tether your horses	In' Wald mit den Rossen
to graze and rest!	zu Rast und Weid'!

ORTLINDE
(also calling into the wood)

See that the mares	Führet die Mähren
are far from the stallions,	fern voneinander,
until our heroes'	bis unsrer Helden
hate has been calmed!	Hass sich gelegt!

(The Valkyries laugh.)

HELMWIGE
(while the others laugh)

My horse has paid	Der Helden Grimm
for the heroes' anger!	büsste schon die Graue!

(renewed laughter)

ROSSWEISSE, GRIMGERDE
(coming from the wood)

Hoyotoho! Hoyotoho!	Hojotoho! Hojotoho!

THE OTHER SIX VALKYRIES

Be welcome! Be welcome!	Willkommen! Willkommen!

SCHWERTLEITE

Did you hunt as a pair?	Wart ihr Kühnen zu zwei?

GRIMGERDE

We left separately,	Getrennt ritten wir
and met on the way.	und trafen uns heut.

ROSSWEISSE

If we are all assembled,	Sind wir alle versammelt,
then wait no longer:	so säumt nicht lange:
to Walhall hurry away;	[8] nach Walhall brechen wir auf,
Wotan is expecting us there.	Wotan zu bringen die Wal.

HELMWIGE

Eight now are here:	Acht sind wir erst:
one is to come.	eine noch fehlt.

GERHILDE

It's that swarthy Wälsung	Bei dem braunen Wälsung
keeping our Brünnhild.	weilt wohl noch Brünnhild.

WALTRAUTE

Then we must wait	Auf sie noch harren
until she is here:	müssen wir hier:
Brünnhild is father's	Walvater gäb' uns
favourite child,	grimmigen Gruss,
and if we leave her behind ...	säh' ohne sie er uns nahn!

SIEGRUNE
(watching from the look-out point)

Hoyotoho! Hoyotoho!	Hojotoho! Hojotoho!
She's here! She's here!	Hieher! Hieher!
In furious haste	[34] In brünstigem Ritt
see Brünnhilde rides.	jagt Brünnhilde her.

THE EIGHT VALKYRIES
(All hasten to the look-out.)

Hoyotoho! Hoyotoho!	[35] Hojotoho! Hojotoho!
Brünnhilde! Hi!	Brünnhilde! Hei!

(They watch with growing astonishment.) [24]

WALTRAUTE

To the pinewood	Nach dem Tann lenkt sie
she is driving her horse.	das taumelnde Ross.

93

And proud Grane is panting hard!	Wie schnaubt Grane vom schnellen Ritt!

ROSSWEISSE

She's forced him to fly faster than ever!	So jach sah ich nie Walküren jagen!

ORTLINDE

Who's that on her saddle?	Was hält sie im Sattel?

HELMWIGE

That is no man!	Das ist kein Held!

SIEGRUNE

It's a girl, surely.	[30a] Eine Frau führt sie.

GERHILDE

And where was she found?	Wie fand sie die Frau?

SCHWERTLEITE

She gives no greeting to her sisters!	Mit keinem Gruss grüsst sie die Schwestern!

WALTRAUTE
(*calling down*)

Hiaha! Brünnhilde! Answer our call!	Heiaha! Brünnhilde! Hörst du uns nicht?

ORTLINDE

Help our sister to leave the saddle!	Helft der Schwester vom Ross sich schwingen!

HELMWIGE, GERHILDE, SIEGRUNE, ROSSWEISSE

Hoyotoho! Hoyotoho!	[35] Hojotoho! Hojotoho!

ORTLINDE, WALTRAUTE, GRIMGERDE, SCHWERTLEITE

Hiaha!	Heiaha!

(*Gerhilde and Schwertleite run into the wood. Siegrune and Rossweisse follow them.*)

WALTRAUTE
(*looking into the wood*)

And powerful Grane has fallen!	Zugrunde stürzt Grane, der starke!

GRIMGERDE

While our sister lifts the girl to the ground!	Aus dem Sattel hebt sie hastig das Weib!

ORTLINDE, WALTRAUTE, GRIMGERDE, SCHWERTLEITE

Sister, sister! What have you done?	Schwester, Schwester! Was ist geschehn?

(*All the Valkyries return to the stage; with them comes Brünnhilde, supporting and leading Sieglinde.*)

BRÜNNHILDE
(*breathless*)

Shield me and help in highest need!	Schützt mich und helft in höchster Not!

THE EIGHT VALKYRIES

From where have you come in furious haste? You ride like one who is pursued!	Wo rittest du her in rasender Hast? So fliegt nur, wer auf der Flucht!

I flee for the first time;	Zum erstenmal flieh ich
I am pursued;	und bin verfolgt:
Wotan is hunting me!	Heervater hetzt mir nach!

THE EIGHT VALKYRIES
(*violently alarmed*)

What are you saying?	Bist du von Sinnen?
Speak to us! What?	Sprich! Sage uns! Wie?
Is Wotan hunting you?	Verfolgt dich Heervater?
Why do you flee?	Fliehst du vor ihm?

BRÜNNHILDE
(*She turns anxiously to look around, and then turns back.*)

O sisters, run	O Schwestern, späht
to the mountain summit!	von des Felsens Spitze!
Look to the northward,	Schaut nach Norden,
if Wotan is near!	ob Walvater naht!

(*Ortlinde and Waltraute run to the rocky peak to keep a look-out.*)

Quick! What can you see?	Schnell! Seht ihr ihn schon?

[24]

ORTLINDE

A thunderstorm	Gewittersturm
nears from northward.	naht von Norden.

WALTRAUTE

Dark, stormy clouds	Starkes Gewölk
mass themselves there!	staut sich dort auf!

THE OTHER SIX VALKYRIES

Wotan is riding	Heervater reitet
his sacred horse!	sein heiliges Ross!

BRÜNNHILDE

The wild pursuer	Der wilde Jäger,
who hunts me in wrath,	der wütend mich jagt,
he's near, he comes from northward.	er naht, er naht von Norden!
Save me, sisters!	Schützt mich, Schwestern!
Rescue this maid!	Wahret dies Weib!

SIX VALKYRIES

But who is this woman?	Was ist mit dem Weibe?

BRÜNNHILDE

Hear while I tell you.	Hört mich in Eile:
Sieglinde is she,	Sieglinde ist es,
Siegmund's sister and bride,	Siegmunds Schwester und Braut:
one of the Wälsungs	Gegen die Wälsungen
Wotan swore to destroy.	wütet Wotan in Grimm;
Her brother's death	dem Bruder sollte
was Brünnhilde's task,	Brünnhilde heut
So Wotan decreed.	entziehen den Sieg;
But Siegmund gained my help	doch Siegmund schützt' ich
in his fight;	mit meinem Schild,
Wotan himself	trotzend dem Gott;
then shattered the sword with the spear:	der traf ihn da selbst mit dem Speer:
Siegmund fell,	Siegmund fiel;
but I fled	doch ich floh
here with his wife,	fern mit der Frau;
and to save her	sie zu retten,
brought her to you.	eilt' ich zu euch
Will you help us both,	ob mich Bange auch
and save us from the storm that is near?	ihr berget vor dem strafenden Streich!

SIX VALKYRIES

What madness moved you
to do this deed?
Sister! Brünnhilde! Sister!
Woe! O rebellious
Brünnhilde,
how could you break his command!

Betörte Schwester,
was tatest du?
Wehe, Brünnhilde, wehe!
Brach ungehorsam
Brünnhilde
Heervaters heilig Gebot?

WALTRAUTE
(*on the look-out*)

Dark those stormclouds
that fly from the north.

[24] Nächtig zieht es
von Norden heran.

ORTLINDE
(*also on the look-out*)

Wotan drives
his steed through the storm.

Wütend steuert
hieher der Sturm.

ROSSWEISSE, GRIMGERDE, SCHWERTLEITE

Wild neighs
I hear from his horse —

[5] Wild wiehert
Walvaters Ross.

HELMWIGE, GERHILDE, SIEGRUNE

— snorts and flies on its way!

Schrecklich schnaubt es daher!

BRÜNNHILDE

Woe to this woman
when Wotan arrives;
for she is a Wälsung,
doomed to destruction!
So lend me the fastest
horse that you have,
to save the maid from his wrath!

Wehe der Armen,
wenn Wotan sie trifft:
den Wälsungen allen
droht er Verderben!
Wer leiht mir von euch
das leichteste Ross,
das flink die Frau ihm entführ'?

SIEGRUNE

So you would make us
share in your crime?

Auch uns rätst du
rasenden Trotz?

BRÜNNHILDE

Rossweisse, sister,
lend me your stallion!

Rossweisse, Schwester,
leih mir deinen Renner!

ROSSWEISSE

From Wotan, my horse
refuses to fly.

Vor Walvater floh
der fliegende nie.

BRÜNNHILDE

Helmwige, hear me!

Helmwige, höre!

HELMWIGE

I hear only Wotan.

Dem Vater gehorch ich.

BRÜNNHILDE

Grimgerde! Gerhilde!
Give me your horse!
Schwertleite! Siegrune!
See my dismay!
Oh, now be true,
as I was to you:
rescue this sorrowful maid!

Grimgerde! Gerhilde!
Gönnt mir eu'r Ross!
Schwertleite! Siegrune!
Seht meine Angst!
O, seid mir treu,
wie traut ich euch war:
rettet dies traurige Weib!

SIEGLINDE
(*She has been gazing gloomily and coldly ahead, then gives a start and makes a gesture of rejection as Brünnhilde impulsively embraces her, as if to protect her.*)

Pray suffer no sorrow for me;
all I long for is death!

Nicht sehre dich Sorge um mich:
einzig taugt mir der Tod!

O warrior maid,
who asked you to save me?
I might have died
in the field with him;
for perhaps the weapon
that dealt his death,
that killed my Siegmund,
had pierced me too.
Far from Siegmund,
Siegmund, from you!
Now only death
can unite us!
So I shall curse
this care that has saved me
if you refuse my grievous entreaty:
strike with your sword in my heart!

Wer hiess dich, Maid,
dem Harst mich entführen?
Im Sturm dort hätt' ich
den Streich empfahn
von derselben Waffe,
der Siegmund fiehl:
das Ende fand ich
vereint mit ihm!
Fern von Siegmund —
Siegmund, von dir! —
O deckte mich Tod,
dass ich's denke!
Soll um die Flucht
dir, Maid, ich nicht fluchen,
so erhöre heilig mein Flehen:
stosse dein Schwert mir ins Herz!

BRÜNNHILDE

Live still, O maid;
know that love commands you!
Rescue the son
who will grow from your love:
a Wälsung lives in your womb!

Lebe, o Weib,
um der Liebe willen!
Rette das Pfand,
das von ihm du empfingst:
ein Wälsung wächst dir im Schoss!

SIEGLINDE
(*She starts in fear at first; then her face lights up with sublime joy.*)

Rescue me, brave one!
Rescue my child!
Save me, you maidens,
and shelter my son!

Rette mich, Kühne!
Rettet mein Kind!
Schirmt mich, ihr Mädchen,
mit mächtigstem Schutz!

(*An ever-darkening tempest rises in the background; the thunder draws closer.*) [24]

WALTRAUTE
(*on the look-out*)

The storm's drawing near!

Der Sturm kommt heran.

ORTLINDE
(*on the look-out*)

Fly if you fear it!

Flieh, wer ihn fürchtet!

THE OTHER SIX VALKYRIES

Off with the woman!
Danger is near!
The Valkyries dare not
give her their aid.

Fort mit dem Weibe,
droht ihm Gefahr:
der Walküren keine
wag ihren Schutz!

SIEGLINDE
(*on her knees to Brünnhilde*)

Rescue me, maid!
Rescue a mother!

Rette mich, Maid!
Rette die Mutter!

BRÜNNHILDE
(*She raises Sieglinde with sudden resolution.*)

Then fly from him swiftly,
and fly by yourself!
I will stay for the storm;
I will brave Wotan's anger;
and I'll draw his revenge
on myself,
so that you can escape his rage.

So fliehe denn eilig
und fliehe allein!
Ich bleibe zurück,
biete mich Wotans Rache:
an mir zögr' ich
den Zürnenden hier,
während du seinem Rasen entrinnst.

[24]

SIEGLINDE

Ah, where can I escape him?

Wohin soll ich mich wenden?

BRÜNNHILDE

Which of you, sisters, journeyed to eastward?	Wer von euch Schwestern schweifte nach Osten?

SIEGRUNE

A gloomy forest lies to the east, where the Nibelung hoard was brought by Fafner, the giant.	Nach Osten weithin dehnt sich ein Wald: der Nibelungen Hort entführte Fafner dorthin.

SCHWERTLEITE

A gloomy forest
lies to the east,
where the Nibelung hoard
was brought by Fafner, the giant.

[6] Wurmesgestalt
schuf sich der Wilde:
in einer Höhle
hütet er Alberichs Reif!

There he remains,
changed to a dragon,
and in a cave
he broods over Alberich's ring.

GRIMGERDE

It is not the place
for a helpless maid.

[21] Nicht geheu'r ist's dort
für ein hilflos Weib.

BRÜNNHILDE

And yet, from Wotan's wrath,
there, I know, she'd be safe:
for father fears it;
he never goes near.

Und doch vor Wotans Wut
schützt sie sicher der Wald:
ihn scheut der Mächt'ge
und meidet den Ort.

WALTRAUTE
(on the look-out) [24]

Angry Wotan
rides to the rock!

Furchtbar fährt
dort Wotan zum Fels.

SIX VALKYRIES

Brünnhilde, hear
his approach in the storm!

Brünnhilde, hör
seines Nahens Gebraus!

BRÜNNHILDE
(showing Sieglinde the direction)

Fly him swiftly,
away to the east!
Bold in defiance,
endure every ill,
hunger and thirst,
thorns and the stones;
laugh at the pain
and grief that will come!
But one thing know,
and guard it ever:
the noblest hero of all,
he shall be born,
O maid, from your womb!

Fort denn eile,
nach Osten gewandt!
Mutigen Trotzes
ertrag alle Müh'n,
Hunger und Durst,
Dorn und Gestein;
[30a] lache, ob Not,
ob Leiden dich nagt!
Denn eines wiss'
und wahr' es immer:
[39] den hehrsten Helden der Welt
hegst du, o Weib,
im schirmenden Schoss!

(*She draws the pieces of Siegmund's sword from beneath her breastplate and gives them to Sieglinde.*) [27]

For him you must guard
these broken pieces
of the sword his father
let fall when it failed him;
for he shall forge
the sword once more.
His name, now learn it from me:
Siegfried — victorious and free!

Verwahr ihm die starken
Schwertesstücken;
seines Vaters Walstatt
entführt' ich sie glücklich:
[39] der neugefügt
das Schwert einst schwingt,
den Namen nehm er von mir —
'Siegfried' erfreu sich des Siegs!

[27]

SIEGLINDE
(deeply stirred)

O radiant wonder!
Glorious maid!

[40] O hehrstes Wunder!
Herrlichste Maid!

Your words have brought me	Dir Treuen dank ich
comfort and calm!	heiligen Trost!
This son of Siegmund, [39]	Für ihn, den wir liebten,
Oh! we shall save him:	rett ich das Liebste:
may my son return	meines Dankes Lohn
to thank you himself!	lache dir einst!
Fare you well!	Lebe wohl!
Be blessed by Sieglinde's woe!	Dich segnet Sieglindes Weh!

(She hastens away in the right foreground. Black thunderclouds surround the height; a fearful storm breaks out at the back, with a fiery glare growing brighter on the right.) [5]

WOTAN'S VOICE

Stay, Brünnhild!	Steh, Brünnhild!

(Brünnhilde, after watching Sieglinde's departure for a while, turns to the background, looks into the pinewood, and then comes forward again in fear.)

ORTLINDE, WALTRAUTE
(descending from the look-out)

They've reached the mountain,	Den Fels erreichten
horse and rider!	Ross und Reiter!

ALL EIGHT VALKYRIES

Woe, Brünnhild!	Weh, Brünnhild!
Vengeance is here!	Rache entbrennt!

BRÜNNHILDE

O sisters, help!	Ach, Schwestern, helft!
I feel afraid! [24]	Mir schwankt das Herz!
His rage will crush me	Sein Zorn zerschellt mich,
unless you shield me from harm.	wenn euer Schutz ihn nicht zähmt.

THE EIGHT VALKYRIES
(They retreat in fear up the rocky height, drawing Brünnhilde with them.)

Come here, you lost one!	Hieher, Verlorne!
Keep out of sight!	Lass dich nicht sehn!
Hide among us here;	Schmiege dich an uns
be still when he calls!	und scheige dem Ruf!

(They hide Brünnhilde in their midst and look anxiously at the pinewood, now lit by a brilliant fiery glow, while the background has become quite dark.)

Woe!	Weh!
Wotan swings himself	Wütend schwingt sich
to the ground!	Wotan von Ross!
Here he comes	Hieher rast
in furious haste!	sein rächender Schritt!

Scene Two. *Wotan comes from the pinewood in a towering rage and strides to the group of Valkyries on the height, looking around for Brünnhilde.* [8]

WOTAN

Where is Brünnhild?	Wo ist Brünnhild,
Where is the guilty one?	wo die Verbrecherin?
Can you be daring	Wagt ihr, die Böse
to hide her from me?	vor mir zu bergen?

THE EIGHT VALKYRIES

Fearful your cry of anger!	Schrecklich ertost dein Toben!
O father, pity your daughters;	Was taten, Vater, die Töchter,
have we awakened	dass sie dich reizten
your terrible rage?	zu rasender Wut?

WOTAN

Ha, so you mock me?	Wollt ihr mich höhnen?
Insolent daughters!	Hütet euch, Freche!
I know Brünnhilde	Ich weiss: Brünnhilde
hides in your midst.	bergt ihr vor mir.

Leave her alone,
for she is an outcast,
and all her virtue
is cast away!

Weichet von ihr,
der ewig Verworfnen,
wie ihren Wert
von sich sie warf!

[36]

ROSSWEISSE

She came here to escape you.

Zu uns floh die Verfolgte.

ALL EIGHT VALKYRIES

And she asked for our help!
In fear and anguish
fled from your rage.
For our trembling sister
now we implore:
let the angry storm now be calm.
Father, have mercy on her,
calm your dreadful rage!

Unsern Schutz flehte sie an!
Mit Furcht und Zagen
fasst sie dein Zorn:
für die bange Schwester
bitten wir nun,
dass den ersten Zorn du bezähmst.
Lass dich erweichen für sie,
zähme deinen Zorn!

WOTAN

Weak-spirited,
womanish brood!
Such whining ways
you learnt not from me!
I tempered your frames
to fight on the field,
made you hard-hearted
and stern and strong:
must I hear you all whine and wail
when I punish a treacherous crime?
I'll tell you, whimperers,
what she has done,
that shameless sister
who has prompted your tears:
Brünnhild alone
knew all my innermost secrets;
Brünnhild alone
saw to the depths of my spirit!
Through her
all my desires took shape in the world:
yet she has broken
the bond of our love,
and, faithless,
she has defied my desire;
my sacred command
openly scorned;
against me lifted the spear
that by Wotan's will she bore!
Hear me, Brünnhilde!
You whom I fashioned,
you who owe
all that you are,
name, even life, to me!
Say, can you hear me accuse you
and hide yourself, you coward,
to try to escape your doom?

Weichherziges
Weibergezücht!
So matten Mut
gewannt ihr von mir?
Erzog ich euch kühn,
zum Kampfe zu ziehn,
schuf ich die Herzen
euch hart und scharf,
dass ihr Wilden nun weint und greint,
[36] wenn mein Grimm eine Treulose straft?
So wisst denn, Winselnde,
was sie verbrach,
um die euch Zagen
die Zähre entbrennt:
Keine wie sie
kannte mein innerstes Sinnen:
keine wie sie
wusste den Quell meines Willens!
Sie selbst war
meines Wunsches schaffender Schoss:
und so nun brach sie
den seligen Bund,
dass treulos sie
meinem Willen getrozt,
mein herrschend Gebot
offen verhöhnt,
gegen mich die Waffe gewandt,
die mein Wunsch allein ihr schuf!
Hörst du's, Brünnhilde?
Du, der ich Brünne,
Helm und Wehr,
Wonne und Huld,
Namen und Leben verlieh?
Hörst du mich Klage erheben
und birgst dich bang dem Kläger,
dass feig du der Straf' entflöst?

BRÜNNHILDE

(*She steps out from the crowd of Valkyries and advances with humble yet resolute steps down the rock, close to Wotan.*) [36]

Here am I, father;
now tell me my sentence!

Hier bin ich, Vater:
gebiete die Strafe!

WOTAN

I sentence you not:
you have brought your doom on yourself.

Nicht straf ich dich erst:
deine Strafe schufst du dir selbst.

100

My will alone
woke you to life,
and against that will you have worked.
By my commandments
alone you could act,
and against me you have commanded.
Brünnhild
knew my wish,
and against that wish she rebelled.
Brünnhild
bore my shield,
and against me that shield was borne.
Brünnhild
could choose my fate,
and she chose that fate was against me.
Once I said to her:
Rouse my men,
and she roused a hero against me.
Though once you were
all that I made you,
what you have become
you choose for yourself!
No more child of my will;
Valkyrie are you no longer;
Henceforth remain
what you chose to be!

Durch meinen Willen
warst du allein:
gegen ihn doch hast du gewollt;
meinen Befehl nur
führtest du aus:
gegen ihn doch hast du befohlen;
Wunschmaid
warst du mir:
gegen mich doch hast du gewünscht;
Schildmaid
warst du mir:
gegen mich doch hobst du den Schild;
Loskieserin
warst du mir:
gegen mich doch kiestest du Lose;
Heldenreizerin
warst du mir:
[9,36]gegen mich doch reiztest du Helden.
Was sonst du warst,
sagte dir Wotan,
was jetzt du bist,
das sage dir selbst!
Wunschmaid bist du nicht mehr,
Walküre bist du gewesen:
nun sei fortan,
was so du noch bist!

BRÜNNHILDE
(*violently terrified*)

So you cast me off?
Is that what you mean?

Du verstössest mich?
Versteh ich den Sinn?

WOTAN

No more will you ride from Walhall;
no more will you choose
heroes who fall;
or bring me the warriors
who guard my hall;
and in Walhall, when we are feasting,
no more shall you fill
my drink-horn for me;
no more may I kiss
the mouth of my child;
the host of the gods
no more shall know you;
cast for ever
from the clan of the gods.
You broke the bond of our love,
and from my sight, henceforth, Brünnhild
is banned!

Nicht send ich dich mehr aus Walhall;
[37]   nicht weis ich dir mehr
Helden zur Wal;
nicht führst du mehr Sieger
in meinen Saal:
bei der Götter trautem Mahle
das Trinkhorn nicht reichst
du traulich mir mehr;
nicht kos ich dir mehr
den kindischen Mund.
Von göttlicher Schar
bist du geschieden,
ausgestossen
aus der Ewigen Stamm;
[9]   gebrochen ist unser Bund;
aus meinem Angesicht bist du verbannt.

THE EIGHT VALKYRIES
(*In consternation, they leave their former position, coming somewhat lower down the rock.*)

Horror! Woe!
Sister, oh sister!

Wehe! Weh!
Schwester, ach Schwester!

BRÜNNHILDE

Can you deprive me
of all you gave?

Nimmst du mir alles,
was einst du gabst?

WOTAN

He who comes robs you of all!
For here on the rock,
here you must stay;
defenceless in sleep,
here you will lie;

[5]   Der dich zwingt, wird dir's entziehn!
Hieher auf den Berg
banne ich dich;
in wehrlosen Schlaf
[9]   schliess ich dich fest:

101

and you'll belong to the man	der Mann dann fange die Maid,
who can find you and wake you from sleep.	der am Wege sie findet und weckt.

THE EIGHT VALKYRIES

(They descend completely from the rocky height, in great consternation, and in anxious groups surround Brünnhilde, who lies half-kneeling before Wotan.)

Ah no, father!		Halt ein, o Vater,	
Recall the curse!		halt ein den Fluch!	
Shall our sister bend	[37]	Soll die Maid verblühn	
to the will of a man?		und verbleichen dem Mann?	
Endless disgrace!		Hör unser Flehn!	
Stern-hearted God!		Schrecklicher Gott,	
Ah, spare her,		wende von ihr	
spare her the shame!	[5]	die schreiende Schmach!	
For our sister's shame on us then would fall!		Wie die Schwester träfe uns selber der Schimpf.	

[24]

WOTAN

Did you not hear		Hörtet ihr nicht,	
what I decreed?	[9]	was ich verhängt?	
that from your band		Aus eurer Schar	
your treacherous sister is banished?		ist die treulose Schwester geschieden;	
No more shall she ride		mit euch zu Ross	
through clouds with her sisters to battle;		durch die Lüfte nicht reitet sie länger;	
the flower of her beauty		die magdliche Blume	
will fade and die;		verblüht der Maid;	
a husband will gain		ein Gatte gewinnt	
all her womanly grace;		ihre weibliche Gunst;	
that masterful husband		dem herrischen Manne	
will make her obey;		gehorcht sie fortan;	
she'll sit and spin by the fire,	[9]	am Herde sitzt sie und spinnt,	
and the world will deride her fate!		aller Spottenden Ziel und Spiel.	

(Brünnhilde sinks with a cry to the ground; the Valkyries, in great agitation, shrink in horror from her side.) [34, 36]

Are you afraid?	Schreckt euch ihr Los?
Then flee from the lost one!	So flieht die Verlorne!
Leave her alone,	Weichet von ihr
and never return!	und haltet euch fern!
If one of you	Wer von euch wagte,
should come to console her,	bei ihr zu weilen,
if she should dare	wer mir zum Trotz
to defy my command,	zu der Traurigen hielt',
that rash one shares in her fate:	die Törin teilte ihr Los:
so now from this peak be gone!	das künd ich der Kühnen an!
Off with you now!	Fort jetzt von hier!
Do not go near her!	Meidet den Felsen!
Ride away from this mountain,	Hurtig jagt mir von hinnen,
or the same fate shall be yours!	sonnst erharrt Jammer euch hier!

THE EIGHT VALKYRIES

Woe! Woe!	Weh! Weh!

(They separate with loud cries of distress and fly in haste into the wood. Black clouds gather on the cliffs; a wild tumult is heard in the wood. A vivid flash of lightning breaks through the clouds; in it are seen the Valkyries, close-grouped, their bridles hanging loose, riding wildly away. [34] The storm soon subsides; the thunderclouds gradually disperse. During the following scene, in increasingly calm weather, twilight falls, and finally night.)

Scene Three. *Wotan and Brünnhilde, who still lies at his feet, are left alone. A long solemn silence: their positions remain unchanged.* [41, 36, 38]

BRÜNNHILDE

(She begins slowly to raise her head a little; beginning timidly and becoming more confident)

Was it so shameful,	[41]	War es so schmählich,
what I have done,		was ich verbrach,

that you must punish my deed with endless shame? [9]	dass mein Verbrechen so schmählich du bestrafst?
Was it disgraceful, what I have done,	War es so niedrig, was ich dir tat,
do I deserve to be plunged in disgrace?	dass du so tief mir Erniedrigung schaffst?
Was my dishonour boundless and base,	War es so ehrlos, was ich beging,
for that offence must my honour be lost?	dass mein Vergehn nun die Ehre mir raubt?

(She raises herself gradually to a kneeling position.) [36, 38]

Oh speak, father!	O sag, Vater!
Look in my eyes:	Sieh mir ins Auge:
silence your scorn,	schweige den Zorn,
soften your wrath,	zähme die Wut
explain to me	und deute mir hell
all the grievous guilt	die dunkle Schuld,
that compels you, cruel and harsh,	die mit starrem Trotze dich zwingt,
to abandon your true, loving child.	zu verstossen dein trautestes Kind!

[36]

WOTAN
(in unchanged attitude, gravely and gloomily)

Ask what you did;	Frag deine Tat,
your deed will tell you your guilt!	sie deutet dir deine Schuld!

[34]

BRÜNNHILDE

By your command	Deinen Befehl
bravely I fought.	führte ich aus.

WOTAN

Did I command you	[8] Befahl ich dir,
to fight for the Wälsung?	[38] für den Wälsung zu fechten?
	[9]

BRÜNNHILDE

That was your command,	So hiessest du mich
as master of fate.	als Herrscher der Wal!

WOTAN

But that command	Doch meine Weisung
you knew I later recalled!	nahm ich wieder zurück!

BRÜNNHILDE

When Fricka had made you	Als Fricka den eignen
change your decision;	Sinn dir entfremdet;
and when her words conquered your will,	da ihrem Sinn du dich fügtest,
you were false to yourself. [36]	warst du selber dir Feind.

WOTAN
(softly and bitterly)

Yet you understood me fully;	Dass du mich verstanden, wähnt' ich
I warned of my rage if you failed;	und strafte den wissenden Trotz:
but no, you thought: [36]	doch feig und dumm
Wotan is weak!	dachtest du mich!
A treacherous crime must be punished;	So hätt' ich Verrat nicht zu rächen,
else on you I'd not waste my rage. [41]	zu gering wärst du meinem Grimm!

BRÜNNHILDE

I know so little	Nicht weise bin ich,
but one thing I did know,	doch wusst' ich das eine,
that the Wälsung you loved.	dass den Wälsung du liebtest.
I saw all your torment, [37]	Ich wusste den Zwiespalt,
as you tried	der dich zwang,
to force yourself to forget this. [31, 36]	dies eine ganz zu vergessen.
The other thing	Das andre musstest
was all you could see,	einzig du sehn,

and the sight of that
tortured your heart:
that Siegmund could not be shielded.

was zu schaun so herb
schmerzte dein Herz:
dass Siegmund Schutz du versagtest.

WOTAN

You knew that was so,
and yet you went to his help?

Du wusstest es so
und wagtest dennoch den Schutz?

BRÜNNHILDE
(*beginning softly*)

Yes, because my eyes
saw but one thing alone,
one all-conquering fact
that you would not face;
you turned your back in your sorrow!
I who guard your back
when you fight in the field,
I saw that one thing
which you could not:
Siegmund I beheld.
I said
you had marked him for death;
I gazed in his eyes then,
heard his reply;
and I shared that hero's
grief and distress,
hearing the call
of his brave lamentation —
love's holy yearning,
hopeless despair —
proud in defiance,
dauntless in grief!
In my ears it rang;
my eyes were dazzled;
my mind was troubled;
a new emotion stole through my heart.
Shy, astonished,
I stood ashamed.
How could I help him,
how could I save him?
Victory or death,
with Siegmund I'd share it!
One thought possessed me,
and I had no choice!
You, who this love
in my heart inspired,
when you inspired
the Wälsung with your will,
you were not betrayed —
though I broke your command.

Weil für dich im Auge
das eine ich hielt,
dem, im Zwange des andren
schmerzlich entzweit,
ratlos den Rücken du wandtest!
Die im Kampfe Wotan
den Rücken bewacht,
die sah nun das nur,
[38] was du nicht sahst:
[37] Siegmund musst' ich sehn.
Tod kündend
trat ich vor ihn,
gewahrte sein Auge,
hörte sein Wort;
ich vernahm des Helden
heilige Not!
tönend erklang mir
des Tapfersten Klage:
freiester Liebe
furchtbares Leid,
[30a] traurigsten Mutes
mächtigster Trotz!
Meinem Ohr erscholl,
mein Aug' erschaute,
was tief im Busen das Herz
zu heil'gem Beben mir traf.
Scheu und staunend
stand ich in Scham.
Ihm nur zu dienen
konnt' ich noch denken:
Sieg oder Tod
mit Siegmund zu teilen:
[36] dies nur erkannt' ich
[41] zu kiesen als Los!
Der diese Liebe
mir ins Herz gehaucht,
dem Willen, der
dem Wälsung mich gesellt,
ihm innig vertraut —
trotzt' ich deinem Gebot.

[41]

WOTAN

So you would attempt
what I longed so dearly to do,
but which cruel fate
forbade me to achieve?
So you thought
that love could be captured so lightly,
while burning woe
broke my heart in two,
and terrible grief
awoke my rage;
when, to save creation,
the spring of love
in my tortured heart I imprisoned?
Then, burning with anger,

So tatest du,
was so gern zu tun ich begehrt,
doch was nicht zu tun
die Not zwiefach mich zwang?
So leicht wähntest du
Wonne der Liebe erworben,
wo brennend Weh
in das Herz mir brach,
wo grässliche Not
den Grimm mir schuf,
einer Welt zuliebe
der Liebe Quell
in gequälten Herzen zu hemmen?
Wo gegen mich selber

I turned on myself,
from an anguished weakness
rising in frenzy,
yearning and raging,
I was inspired
and driven to a fearful resolve:
in the wreck of my ruined world
my unending sorrow I'd bury:
  while you lay lapped
in blissful delight,
filled with emotion's
rapturous joy;
you laughed, while drinking
the draught of love,
and I tasted the gall,
drained bitter sorrow and grief!
  You indulged your love;
now let it lead you:
from me you have turned away.
  So I must shun you;
no more may I share
with you my secret counsels;
henceforth our paths
are parted forever:
for, while life shall endure,
I, the god, no more shall behold you.

ich sehrend mich wandte,
aus Ohnmachtsschmerzen
schäumend ich aufschoss,
wütender Sehnsucht
sengender Wunsch
den schrecklichen Willen mir schuf,
in den Trümmern der eignen Welt
[25] meine ew'ge Trauer zu enden:
[23]   da labte süss
dich selige Lust;
wonniger Rührung
üppigen Rausch
enttrankst du lachend
[38]   der Liebe Trank,
als mir göttliche Not
nagende Galle gemischt?
  Deinen leichten Sinn
lass dich denn leiten:
[41] von mir sagtest du dich los.
  Dich muss ich meiden,
gemeinsam mit dir
nicht darf ich Rat mehr raunen;
getrennt nicht dürfen
traut wir mehr schaffen:
so weit Leben und Luft,
[41, 9] darf der Gott dir nicht mehr begegnen!

BRÜNNHILDE

Unworthy of you
this foolish maid,
who, stunned by your counsel,
misunderstood,
when that one command
overruled all the rest:
to love him whom you had loved.
  If I must lose you,
and you must leave me,
if you sever
the bonds that we tied,
then half your being
you have abandoned,
which once belonged to you only.
O god, forget not that!
  That other self
you must not dishonour;
if you disgrace her,
it falls on you:
your fame then would be darkened,
if I were scorned and despised!

Wohl taugte dir nicht
die tör'ge Maid,
die staunend im Rate
nicht dich verstand,
wie mein eigner Rat
nur das eine mir riet:
zu lieben, was du geliebt.
  Muss ich denn scheiden
und scheu dich meiden,
musst du spalten,
was einst sich umspannt,
die eigne Hälfte
fern von dir halten,
dass sonst sie ganz dir gehörte,
du Gott, vergiss das nicht!
  Dein ewig Teil
nicht wirst du entehren,
Schande nicht wollen,
die dich beschimpft:
dich selbst liessest du sinken,
sähst du dem Spott mich zum Spiel!

[30b]

WOTAN

You chose in rapture
the path of love:
follow love's path,
and obey your lord!

Du folgtest selig
der Liebe Macht:
folge nun dem,
den du lieben musst!

BRÜNNHILDE

If I must go from Walhall,
and play no more part in your actions,
and take as my master
some man to obey:
be sure no coward
makes me his prize;
be sure some hero
wins me as bride!

Soll ich aus Walhall scheiden,
nicht mehr mit dir schaffen und walten,
dem herrischen Manne
gehorchen fortan:
dem feigen Prahler
gib mich nicht preis!
Nicht wertlos sei er,
der mich gewinnt.

From Wotan you turned away;
your conqueror I cannot choose.

Von Walvater schiedest du,
nicht wählen darf er für dich.

BRÜNNHILDE
(softly and confidingly) [33]

You fathered a glorious race;
that race cannot bring forth a coward:
a hero will come, I know it;
be born of Wälsung blood.

Du zeugtest ein edles Geschlecht;
kein Zager kann je ihm entschlagen:
[39] der weihlichste Held — ich weiss es —
entblüht dem Wälsungenstamm!

WOTAN

Name not the Wälsungs to me!
By your desertion
the Wälsungs were doomed;
my rage destroys all the race!

Schweig von dem Wälsungenstamm!
Von dir geschieden,
schied ich von ihm:
vernichten musst' ihn der Neid!

BRÜNNHILDE

She who turned from you
rescued the race.
Sieglinde bears
the holiest fruit;
in pain and grief
such as no woman suffered,
she will give birth
to a Wälsung child.

Die von dir sich riss,
[39] rettete ihn.
Sieglinde hegt
die heiligste Frucht;
in Schmerz und Leid,
wie kein Weib sie gelitten,
wird sie gebären,
was bang sie birgt.

WOTAN

I'll offer no help —
neither to her
nor to any Wälsung child.

Nie suche bei mir
[39, 9] Schutz für die Frau,
noch für ihres Schosses Frucht!

BRÜNNHILDE

She still has the sword
that you made for Siegmund.

[27] Sie wahret das Schwert,
das du Siegmund schufest.

WOTAN
(vehemently)

And which I later broke again!
Seek not, O child,
to change my decision;
await now your fate,
as it must fall:
I may not choose it for you!
But now I must go,
far from this place;
too long now I have delayed.
For as you turned from me,
I turn from you;
I may not even
ask what you wish:
your sentence now
I must see fulfilled.

[38] Und das ich ihm in Stücken schlug!
Nicht streb, o Maid,
den Mut mir zu stören;
erwarte dein Los,
wie sich's dir wirft;
nicht kiesen kann ich es dir!
Doch fort muss ich jetzt,
fern mich verziehn;
zuviel schon zögert' ich hier.
Von der Abwendigen
wend ich mich ab;
nicht wissen darf ich,
was sie sich wünscht:
die Strafe nur
muss vollstreckt ich sehn!

BRÜNNHILDE

What have you decreed
that I must suffer?

Was hast du erdacht,
dass ich erdulde?

WOTAN

In long, deep sleep
you shall be bound:
the man who wakes you again,
that man awakes you as wife!

[42] In festen Schlaf
[8] verschliess ich dich:
wer so die Wehrlose weckt,
dem ward, erwacht, sie zum Weib!

BRÜNNHILDE
(*falls on her knees*)

If fetters of sleep	Soll fesselnder Schlaf
come to bind me,	fest mich binden,
if I must fall	dem feigsten Manne
to the man who finds me, [43]	zur leichten Beute:
then one thing more you must grant me;	dies eine musst du erhören,
in deepest anguish I pray!	was heil'ge Angst zu dir fleht!
Oh shelter my slumber,	Die Schlafende schütze
protect me with terrors,	mit scheuchendem Schrecken,
let only one [39]	dass nur ein furchtlos
who is fearless and free,	freiester Held
none but a hero	hier auf dem Felsen
find me here!	einst mich fänd'!
[43]	

WOTAN

Too much you are asking,	Zuviel begehrst du,
too great a grace.	zuviel der Gunst!

BRÜNNHILDE
(*embracing his knees*)

This one thing more	Dies eine
you must grant me!	musst du erhören!
Oh kill me at once	Zerknicke dein Kind,
as I clasp your knee;	das dein Knie umfasst;
destroy your daughter,	zertritt die Traute,
condemn me to die,	zertrümmre die Maid,
let my breast receive	ihres Leibes Spur
one blow from your spear; [9]	zerstöre dein Speer:
but ah! cast not this shame,	doch gib, Grausamer, nicht
this cruel disgrace on me!	der grässlichsten Schmach sie preis!

(*with wild inspiration*) [34]

At your command	Auf dein Gebot
a flame can be kindled, [14]	entbrenne ein Feuer;
a fiery guardian,	den Felsen umglühe
girding the rock, [42]	lodernde Glut;
to lick with its tongues,	es leck ihre Zung',
to tear with its teeth	es fresse ihr Zahn
the craven who rashly ventures,	den Zagen, der frech sich wagte,
who dares to approach near the rock!	dem freislichen Felsen zu nahn!
[39]	

WOTAN
(*overcome and deeply moved, turns eagerly towards Brünnhilde, raises her from her knees and gazes with emotion into her eyes.*) [34, 43]

Farewell, my valiant,	Leb wohl, du kühnes,
glorious child!	herrliches Kind!
You were the holiest pride of my heart!	Du meines Herzens heiligster Stolz!
Farewell! Farewell! Farewell!	Leb wohl! Leb wohl! Leb wohl!

(*very passionately*)

Though I must leave you,	Muss ich dich meiden,
and may no longer	und darf nicht minnig
embrace you in greeting;	mein Gruss dich mehr grüssen;
though you may no more	sollst du nun nicht mehr
ride beside me,	neben mir reiten,
nor bear my mead in Walhall;	noch Met beim Mahl mir reichen;
though I abandon you	muss ich verlieren
whom I love so,	dich, die ich liebte,
the laughing delight of my eye:	du lachende Lust meines Auges:
a bridal fire [42]	ein bräutliches Feuer
shall blaze to protect you,	soll dir nun brennen,
as never has burned for a bride.	wie nie einer Braut es gebrannt!
Threatening flames [14]	Flammende Glut
shall flare from the rock;	umglühe den Fels;
the craven will fear it, [42]	mit zehrenden Schrecken

107

cringe from its fury;
the weak will flee
from Brünnhilde's rock!
For one alone wins you as bride,   [39]
one freer than I, the god!   [41, 43]

(Brünnhilde, moved and exalted, sinks on Wotan's breast; he holds her in a long embrace. She throws her head back again and, still embracing him, gazes with solemn rapture into his eyes.)

These radiant, glorious eyes,
which, smiling, often I kissed,
  when courage
  I acclaimed with kisses,
  while childish prattle
  in heroes' praise
so sweetly poured from your lips:
yes, these gleaming, radiant eyes,
which shone so bright in the storm,
  when hopeless yearning
  consumed my spirit,
  and worldly pleasures
  were all I longed for,
when fear fastened upon me —
  their glorious fire
  gladdens me now,
  as I take this loving,
  last farewell!   [43]
On some happy mortal
one day they will shine:
but I, hapless immortal,
I must lose them forever.

(He clasps her head in his hands.) [7]

And sadly
this god must depart;
my kiss takes your godhead away!

[42, 43, 38]

(He presses a long kiss on her eyes. She sinks back with closed eyes, unconscious, in his arms. He gently supports her to a low mossy bank, which is overshadowed by a wide-branching fir tree, and lays her upon it. He looks upon her and closes her helmet; his eye then rests on the form of the sleeper, which he completely covers with the great steel shield of the Valkyrie. He turns slowly away, then turns round again with a sorrowful look. Then he strides with solemn decision to the middle of the stage, and directs the point of his spear towards a massive rock.)

Loge, hear!   [9, 13b]
Come at my call!
As when first you were found,
a fiery glow,
as when then you escaped me,
a wandering flicker;
once you were bound:
be so again!   [9, 14]
Arise! Come, flickering Loge;
surround the rock, ring it with flame!   [13a]

(During the following he strikes the rock three times with his spear.)

Loge! Loge! Appear!   [13b, 14, 13a]

(A flash of flame leaps from the rock, and gradually increases to an ever-brightening fiery glow. Flickering flames break out. Bright, shooting flames surround Wotan. With his spear, he directs the sea of fire to encircle the rocks; it presently spreads towards the background, where it encloses the mountain in flames.) [42, 43]

Only the man   [39]
who braves my spear-point
can pass through this sea of flame!   [38]

(He stretches out the spear as if casting a spell. Then he gazes sorrowfully back at Brünnhilde, turns slowly to depart, and looks back once more before he disappears through the fire. The curtain falls.)

scheuch es den Zagen;
der Feige fliehe
Brünnhildes Fels!
Denn einer nur freie die Braut,
der freier als ich, der Gott!

Der Augen leuchtendes Paar,
das oft ich lächelnd gekost,
  wenn Kampfeslust
  ein Kuss dir lohnte,
  wenn kindisch lallend
  der Helden Lob
von holden Lippen dir floss:
dieser Augen strahlendes Paar,
das oft im Sturm mir geglänzt,
  wenn Hoffnungssehnen
  das Herz mir sengte,
  nach Weltenwonne
  mein Wunsch verlangte
aus wild webendem Bangen:
  zum letztenmal
  letz es mich heut
  mit des Lebewohles
  letztem Kuss!
Dem glücklichern Manne
glänze sein Stern:
dem unseligen Ew'gen
muss es scheidend sich schliessen.

Denn so kehrt
der Gott sich dir ab,
so küsst er die Gottheit von dir!

Loge, hör!
Lausche hieher!
Wie zuerst ich dich fand,
als feurige Glut,
wie dann einst du mir schwandest
als schweifende Lohe;
wie ich dich band,
bann ich dich heut!
Herauf, wabernde Lohe,
umlodre mir feurig den Fels!

Loge! Loge! Hieher!

Wer meines Speeres
Spitze fürchtet,
durchschreite das Feuer nie!

108

Bibliography

Wagner wrote *Eine Mitteilung an meine Freunde* (*A Communication to My Friends*, 1851) as an introduction for them to the new form of *The Ring*. *Oper und Drama* (*Opera and Drama*, 1852) sets out these theories of opera which are best exemplified in *The Valkyrie*. Both essays are included in *The Complete Prose Works of Richard Wagner*, translated by W. Ashton Ellis (London, 1892) which, although neither accurate nor fluent, is the most widely available translation. Robert Hartford's chronicle of *Bayreuth: The Early Years . . . as seen by the celebrated visitors and participants* (London, 1980), and the eye-witness account of the stage rehearsals for the first Bayreuth festival in *Wagner Rehearsing the 'Ring'* by Heinrich Porges (trans. R. Jacobs, Cambridge, 1983) give vivid insights into the first cycles. The two massive volumes of *Cosima Wagner's Diaries* (I, 1869-77; II, 1878-83) make astonishing reading because of their frankness and comprehensiveness (ed. Gregor-Dellin and Mack, trans. G. Skelton, London, 1978, 1980).

There are now a number of relatively modern studies in English devoted to *The Ring*. *Wagner's 'Ring': An Introduction* by Alan Blyth (London, 1980) contains simple musical synopses for the cycle in one compact volume. *I Saw The World End* by Deryck Cooke (Oxford, 1979) and *Wagner's 'Ring' and its Symbols* by Robert Donington (London, 1963) are brilliant and much more densely argued commentaries which have prompted in turn much discussion. Carl Dahlhaus's perceptive *Musicdramas of Richard Wagner* (trans. M. Whittall, Cambridge, 1980) includes chapters on the cycle, and *The Wagner Companion* (ed. Peter Burbidge and Richard Sutton, London, 1979) includes several essays of especial interest.

The Perfect Wagnerite by Bernard Shaw (London, 1898; New York, 1967) and *The Life of Richard Wagner* (London, 1933-47) and *Wagner Nights* (London, 1949) by Ernest Newman are classic introductions to the cycle. The commentary of Paul Bekker in *Richard Wagner, His Life and His Work* (trans. M. Bozman, New York, 1931, 1971) is also still exceptionally rewarding. John Culshaw has written several books about Wagner and his account of recording the Decca *Ring* cycle is of great interest to lovers of the score as well as record enthusiasts: *Ring Resounding* (London, 1967). Geoffrey Skelton's *Wieland Wagner: The Positive Sceptic* is a sympathetic account of Wieland Wagner's productions and ideas. (See also his entry in *Contributors*.) There are shorter biographies by Curt von Westernhagen (Cambridge, 1978) and John Gutman (London, 1968, 1971).

Discography by *Martin Hoyle*. For detailed analysis the enthusiast is referred to *Opera on Record*, ed. Alan Blyth, Hutchinson, 1979. The recordings here listed are in German except where stated.

Conductor Orchestra/Opera House	*Solti* Vienna PO	*Furtwängler* Rome PO	*Karajan* Berlin PO	*Janowski* Dresden Staatskapelle
Wotan	Hotter	Frantz	Stewart	Adam
Siegmund	King	Windgassen	Vickers	Jerusalem
Sieglinde	Crespin	Konetzni	Janowitz	Norman
Brünnhilde	Nilsson	Mödl	Crespin	Altmeyer
Fricka	Ludwig	Cavelti	Veasey	Minton
Hunding	Frick	Frick	Talvela	Moll
Disc UK number	SET 312-6	RLS 702	2740 146	301 143
Tape UK number	K3W30	—	3378 049	—
Excerpts UK (disc)	SET 390	—	—	—
Disc US	Lon 1509	—	2713 002	301 143
Tape US	5-1509	—	3378 049	501 143
Excerpts (US disc)	Lon 26085	—	—	—

Conductor	Boehm	Goodall (in English)	Boulez	Furtwängler
Orchestra/Opera House	Bayreuth	ENO	Bayreuth	La Scala
Wotan	Adam	Bailey	McIntyre	Frantz
Siegmund	King	Remedios	Hofmann	Treptow
Sieglinde	Rysanek	Curphey	Altmeyer	Konetzni
Brünnhilde	Nilsson	Hunter	Jones	Flagstad
Fricka	Burmeister	Howard	Schwarz	Hoengen
Hunding	Nienstedt	Grant	Salminnen	Weber
Disc UK	6747 037	SLS 5063	6769 074	940 477
Tape UK	—	TC-SLS5063	—	—
Excerpts UK	—	—	—	—
Disc US	—	—	6769 071	—
Tape US	—	—	—	—
Excerpts US	—	—	—	—

Contributors

Geoffrey Skelton is the author of *Wagner at Bayreuth: Experiment and Tradition* (London 1965, 2nd ed. 1976), *Wieland Wagner: The Positive Sceptic* (London, 1971), *Richard and Cosima Wagner: Biography of a Marriage* (London, 1982), the translator of *Cosima Wagner's Diaries*, and has written features on Wagnerian subjects for the BBC and South West German Radio.

George Gillespie is Professor of German at University College, Cardiff, and the author of *A Catalogue of Persons Named in German Heroic Literature 700-1600* (Oxford, 1973).

Barry Millington has written music criticism for a number of periodicals, including *The Times* and *Musical Times*. He is currently writing a new Wagner volume for the *Master Musicians* series.

Andrew Porter, translator of many Verdi and Mozart operas as well as *The Ring* and *Tristan and Isolde*, is music critic for *The New Yorker*.

Elizabeth Forbes, author of The Observer's Book of Opera (F. Warne, 1982), writes regularly for *Opera* magazine, *Opera News* and *Opera International*, and has translated librettos from French, German and Swedish.

Grateful acknowledgement is also due to William Mann, Lionel Friend, David Murray, Patrick Carnegy, Timothy McFarland and Jeremy Noble for their advice in the preparation of this book.

The Annunciation of Death as envisaged by Theodor Pixis (Wittelsbacher Ausgleichsfond)